The Technology Garden

The Technology Garden

Cultivating Sustainable IT–Business Alignment

Jon Collins, Neil Macehiter, Dale Vile and Neil Ward-Dutton

John Wiley & Sons, Ltd

Copyright © 2007   Jon Collins, Dale Vile, Neil Macehiter and Neil Ward-Dutton

Published by   John Wiley & Sons Ltd, The Atrium, Southern Gate, Chichester,
                        West Sussex PO19 8SQ, England

                        Telephone (+44) 1243 779777

Email (for orders and customer service enquiries): cs-books@wiley.co.uk
Visit our Home Page on www.wiley.com

Other Wiley Editorial Offices

John Wiley & Sons Inc., 111 River Street, Hoboken, NJ 07030, USA

Jossey-Bass, 989 Market Street, San Francisco, CA 94103-1741, USA

Wiley-VCH Verlag GmbH, Boschstr. 12, D-69469 Weinheim, Germany

John Wiley & Sons Australia Ltd, 42 McDougall Street, Milton, Queensland 4064, Australia

John Wiley & Sons (Asia) Pte Ltd, 2 Clementi Loop #02-01, Jin Xing Distripark, Singapore 129809

John Wiley & Sons Canada Ltd, 22 Worcester Road, Etobicoke, Ontario, Canada M9W 1L1

Wiley also publishes its books in a variety of electronic formats. Some content that appears in print may not be available in
electronic books.

British Library Cataloguing in Publication Data

ISBN-13: 978-0-470-72406-4

Typeset in 10.5/13 pt, Minion, Thomson Digital. India.
Printed and bound in Great Britain by Bell & Brain Glasgow
This book is printed on acid-free paper responsibly manufactured from sustainable forestry
in which at least two trees are planted for each one used for paper production.

Contents

Preface

What is it about Information Technology (IT) that makes it so difficult to deliver? Of course, technology can be difficult and complex, but then, so can be engineering, genetics or any number of other disciplines. As we started developing the ideas in this book, we spent some time thinking about what was going wrong. Indeed, the entire volume could have been about war stories, tales from the front lines of IT failure, but that wouldn't be too helpful. Instead, we turned our cogitations to the causes of that failure and what could be done to address them.

There is frequent talk in computing circles that the mainframe guys had it right in terms of computer design and that very little has been invented since then. While plenty of good might have come out of the 1970s, perhaps one less-than-positive legacy is the notion that computers and other technologies can, in some way, be built to last: Once deployed, they can be left well alone. The last couple of decades have shown us that nothing could be further from the truth; however, many organisations still act as if it were so.

Even the failings of IT are generally bounded within discrete projects – like medieval cathedral builders or motorcar manufacturers, the suggestion is that the end result will somehow be fixed in time. The computing press is full of examples of projects that have failed to deliver, but this attention masks the bigger problem: Even projects delivered to time and to budget deliver a disappointing service and poor returns on the original investment. Perhaps it is a psychological trait, a combination of denial and making do, which leads to the belief that things will be different this time, and that somehow, IT will start to fit the definition of what it should be, rather than what it is known to be.

Reality suggests that IT is not a cathedral, a bridge or a car. Instead, it is a combination of technologies that count more than individual components; the components are constantly evolving and changing, and the combinations are infinite, as they are modified to suit the similarly evolving and changing needs of the business and to exploit the potential of new capabilities. IT must scale all the way up to support the needs of the largest organisations, and still function for the smallest. In this respect, it is more like a garden, in which combinations of technologies are created, sown, nurtured and razed in turn to suit the needs of its occupants.

We set out to discover how to align IT with the business. To do so, we talked to people at the front line of the IT–business interface, with real experience of the failings of technology delivery and the wherewithal to do something about them. In discussions, we uncovered six principles that can be applied by organisations large and small that are struggling to align the investment in and delivery of IT capabilities with business priorities and objectives in the face of ever-rapid business and technology change.

Two common themes permeate the principles and the way they are applied: sustainability and trust. Sustainability – key to any successful garden – is a crucial protection against the risks of the one-shot approaches frequently applied to IT. A lack of sustainability has resulted in not only disappointment but also inordinate waste, as new technology deployments have almost immediately become 'legacy' and, over time, resulted in IT assets being written off before their time. Meanwhile, the outcome of such failings is one of diminished trust: Just as few will venture into an overgrown garden, neither does the business want to engage with IT until it can prove it is an asset to the organisation, not just a drain on resources.

There can be no trust without engagement, without open dialogue. We hope you can benefit from this book whichever side of the IT/business divide you find yourself on, but perhaps the real test is how well it catalyses the conversation between the two sides. We welcome your feedback: Please do visit our site at http://technologygarden.wordpress.com, where you can post any comments you may have.

Jon Collins, Neil Macehiter, Dale Vile and Neil Ward-Dutton

Acknowledgements

This book is a collation of our own experiences, which have been greatly added to by the collective wisdom of a wide variety of people, too many to mention. Special thanks go to our interviewees who we have cited in the text – Sally Bean, Carson Booth, Darin Brumby, Andreas Dietrich, Bob Doyle, Graeme Hackland, John Johnson, Jon Larsen, Nick Malik, Mark McAllister, Dale Nix, Adam Overfield, Thomas Schiller, Richard Steel, Graeme Tozer, Malcolm Whitehouse and Angela Yochem – as well as Stewart Hair of EDS, Yew Jin Kang of MetLife, David Lipsey of Ordnance Survey, James McGovern, and P.K. Sharma of

EDS, all of whose inputs helped us enormously to guide both the content and the structure of the book. Thanks to all of you and to the innumerable others who have guided our thinking and will continue to do so.

In addition, there are a number of sources of thinking that we would like to mention:

- Nicholas Carr for his contrarian views regarding the business value of IT to provide an alternative perspective – http://www.roughtype.com

- Andrew McAfee of the Harvard Business School for his insight into positioning IT in a business context – http://blog.hbs.edu/faculty/amcafee/

- J.P. Rangaswami of British Telecom for helping us to think outside the traditional boundaries of business IT – http://confusedofcalcutta.com

- John Hagel for his thoughts on changing business models – http://www.edgeperspectives.typepad.com/

Beyond the interviewees and helpful sources, we would also like to thank our own partners and families for their forbearance and understanding: Claire and Oscar Ward-Dutton, Sam and Bex Macehiter, Helen, Jack and Laura Vile, and Liz, Ben and Sophie Collins.

About the authors

To create a volume of practical advice, the authors have used a combined experience of over 80 years in Information Technology, from a variety of backgrounds including IT management for end users, IT systems development and sales for vendors, and business and IT consultancy. The authors have worked together in the past, and continue to do so in the present, sharing a remit to cut the Gordian Knot that is at the heart of IT–business alignment.

Jon Collins has nearly 20 years of experience in IT. Jon is the service director of Freeform Dynamics, a leading IT industry research and analysis company. He has worked as an industry analyst for over 7 years, for companies including Quocirca, Bloor Research and IDC. He has acted as an advisor to leading vendors including Cisco, EMC, IBM and Microsoft, and to large IT user organisations in the Government, Telecommunications and Financial Services sectors. Jon speaks regularly at IT conferences and writes columns for a number of trade publications including Silicon.com, The Register and Computer Reseller News. He has an end-user background, having worked as an IT consultant, network manager and software engineer for companies such as Admiral Management Services Ltd, Alcatel and Philips Electronics, respectively.

Dale Vile is one of the founders of Freeform Dynamics, an analyst firm that has built its business around the concept of community based research. This innovative approach is used to harvest specific views and experiences within the broader community of business and IT professionals as a foundation for deriving more general advice and guidance on the effective application of IT in a business environment.

As an active industry analyst, Dale is a prolific writer and his views and opinions are widely published in print and online, reinforced by his extensive experience in both end-user and vendor environments. In the first part of his career, he held positions as developer, architect and project manager, delivering systems for companies such as Glaxo and Heineken. He later moved into the IT vendor community, working in various consulting, business development and management roles at Nortel Networks, SAP, JD Edwards and Sybase.

Dale has worked as an industry analyst since the year 2000, initially with Bloor Research, and later with Quocirca, where he co-managed the initial growth of the organisation, then developed and ran the company's core primary research business until co-founding Freeform Dynamics in 2005.

For further information on Freeform Dynamics, please visit www.freeformdynamics.com.

Neil Macehiter is one of the founders of Macehiter Ward-Dutton, an IT advisory firm focused firmly on the challenge of IT–business alignment. He has almost 21 years of experience in the IT industry, having worked in consulting, product and technology strategy roles for vendors including Oracle, Sybase, Sun Microsystems and Autonomy and as the development manager for a telecommunications provider. Neil joined Ovum's consulting practice advising clients on a variety of IT strategy issues and then became its director of software infrastructure research.

Neil Ward-Dutton is the other founder of Macehiter Ward-Dutton. He has over 15 years of experience in the IT industry – in a mixture of consulting and industry analysis roles. He started his career as a business analyst at ICI, and then spent a number of years as a software engineer working for one of the UK's leading software consultancies at the time, Praxis. Not too long after Praxis was bought by Deloitte Consulting, Neil realised he was best suited to small companies and left to join Ovum as a junior IT industry analyst. In 10 years at Ovum, he rose to direct all the technology research programmes of the company–but his ambition turned to new pastures, and in early 2005 he cofounded Macehiter Ward-Dutton.

For further information on Macehiter Ward-Dutton, please visit www.mwdadvisors.com.

1

Introduction

This book offers a practical guide to you if you want to improve the return your organisation gets from its IT investments and ultimately if you want to use IT to help drive transformation in your organisation. The book distils what we have learned from conversations with practitioners into six common-sense, actionable principles, based on best practices, which you can use to improve alignment between IT and business priorities, goals and strategies.

This book is focused on improving the situation as it stands today. It is not a collection of impractical theories or a set of best practices from a single organisation, which cannot be broadly applied. Throughout, it incorporates a wide variety of examples, covering both where things have worked well and where they have failed, from which you can draw based on your situation.

What on earth has IT got to do with gardening?

If everything in IT was working even mostly as it should be, this book would not be necessary.

As things stand, it is.

IT doesn't matter?

When former Harvard Business Review editor Nicholas Carr posited 'IT Doesn't Matter' in 2003, he was making the point that component technologies are commoditising and thus available to all. It's true that, for established companies (as opposed to 'green fields' such as Google, say), the acquisition of IT confers less in the way of strategic advantage than it used to. It is not like the old days, when you could steal a march on your competition as did, for example, American Airlines with its Sabre reservation system or Dell with its online ordering and fulfilment systems.

However, there is another side to IT, concerning how it can actually prevent organisations from progressing. In many organisations, IT is a bottleneck: it reinforces clunky processes, complicates interpersonal communications and restricts business activities. IT and business activity can be misaligned to such an extent that organisations are forced into bankruptcy. This leads to the question, if IT isn't actually helping the business, what the heck is it there for?

Where we fundamentally agree with Carr is that IT *shouldn't* matter quite so much, in the first instance – given the promise of technology, the fact that it is a bottleneck is a travesty. Many organisations would be delighted if IT became no more than an efficiently run, commoditised platform, since it would be a vast improvement over the hotchpotch of inefficient, legacy technologies they are forced to put up with. And even relatively young companies can quickly find themselves hampered by past technology investments.

Ironically, commoditisation can make things worse, since the same underlying trends that render the strategic business value of core technology marginal illustrate even more starkly the weaknesses in how technology is deployed. Like castles built on sand, new technologies are layered on top of the rather shaky foundation of the old, increasing complexity in the hope that old problems will be resolved, or perhaps concealed by the new. Although the 'what' of IT might be a commodity, the 'how' of IT – and specifically 'how' it is employed in the support of business initiatives and functions – absolutely does matter. As the utilisation of technology within organisations becomes more and more complicated, the focus needs to move away from the 'what' and towards the 'how'.

This is as true for public organisations as it is for private companies. Public bodies differentiate themselves on the basis of the services they deliver to their constituencies: should they fail, they can be reorganised into oblivion. More and more public agencies must operate in the same way as commercial businesses: indeed, there are a number of examples in this book of how it is in their best interests to look for commercial opportunities. But first, of course, they need to get on top of their costs and use IT to support the existing services, without which commercial potential is no more than that, potential.

We need to treat the ecosystem

The killer is that although individual technologies might not matter, business value is both realised through and constrained by the orchestrated operation of the whole ecosystems of technologies and service providers. The goal of this book, therefore, is twofold. First, it sets out to help you reduce the waste, minimise the problems and achieve a state of improved business alignment – that is, where your IT capability matches up with your business needs. In other words, it shifts IT from being a bottleneck to being a foundation, as shown in the first two steps of Figure 1.1.

Having done this, it is then possible to determine how IT can make a real difference to the business (the final step in Fig. 1.1), above and beyond the competition – IT as a differentiator. We're not looking to turn everyone into Google. Rather, we believe that organisations have the opportunity to improve above and beyond what is considered the norm. Only once you have escaped from the primeval swamp of legacy IT, are you in a position to use it to your advantage – and in this, you have as much chance of success as anybody else.

Our research – both gained as a result of a collective 80 years in the IT industry and specifically conducted for this book – strongly suggests that the knowledge, tactics and strategies that comprise the 'how' are far from commodities. There are pockets of best practices, but there are vast expanses of corporate space where the relationships between

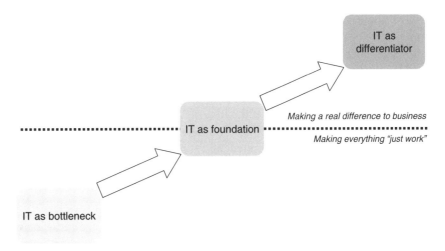

Figure 1.1: IT transformation

IT investments and their business environments are highly dysfunctional. Often, this is as much a result of business organisation dysfunction as IT dysfunction: to succeed, both must be treated at once.

Entering the technology garden

There's something about a garden. Stand in the middle of one and it will tell you a story, about its purpose and intentions, its current state and perhaps most importantly, who looks after it. One thing that will be immediately apparent – so obvious; in fact, it almost goes without saying – is that it will be different from one day to the next.

A garden is not fixed in time. There are too many influences, too many factors – from the weather to invasions of parasites – that can change and impact its state. Not only are its individual components in a constant state of growth – or, indeed, death – but each component can also impact everything else, so a leafy tree in summer prevents things from growing beneath it, or a climbing plant, left unkempt, quickly overcomes its neighbours. Also, seasonal effects stimulate their own cycles of new growth, as plants, trees and shrubs blossom, cross-pollinate and go back into wintry hibernation. Every day, sun and rain cause change – living in Britain we are only too aware how unpredictable the weather can be and the unexpected effects it can have.

We know all of this to such an extent, in fact, that we accept it without question and deal with the consequences: prune before the spring; don't plant in the shade; keep on top of the weeds. Everything from soil to sap is dealt with as part of the whole, as all must function together.

Technology components are not plants: we have not yet invented self-building robots or self-modifying code. However, it is the gardening state of mind that is so lacking in today's IT organisations. As mentioned in the preface, there is a tendency to persist with the idea that technology, once implemented, should just work – even though we know it is a false premise. Instead, there is an urgent need to adopt a very different model for how IT capabilities are defined, deployed and managed.

In this book, we focus a great deal on the idea of 'services'. To explain what these are, consider how many times you have heard someone exclaim, 'I don't know why they make these mobile phones so complicated, all I want to do is make phone calls!' While a phone may be technologically complex, that is no excuse to lose sight of its primary purpose – to enable voice calls. That is the difference between technology and service.

While technology components may be fixed, services most certainly are not. They, like plants, are dependent on context, can grow and diminish in importance as the 'seasons' of a business change from investment, to growth or consolidation. Services can restrict each other's capabilities. And, like plants, services have a lifecycle. They are created, developed, maintained, and ultimately, they die, but the garden as a whole is sustainable, if it is tended correctly.

Above all, that is where the 'garden' paradigm makes the most sense. In our research for this book, we have learned a great deal about how organisations successfully achieve and sustain alignment between IT and the business. If sustainability is the goal, it is services that must be cultivated, whatever the underlying technology foundation.

So, look around your organisation. Do you consider your IT capabilities in terms of services? Do you understand their purpose and their current state and what is expected of them? Most of all, what do they tell you about who looks after them? If all you see is an overgrown mess, all is not lost – even the most chaotic gardens can be rescued from chaos and returned to their former glory, or indeed, made comparable to the best.

The technology garden provides organisations large and small with the opportunity to get on top of IT and to make it work for them. As we are naturally inclined to be positive about the potential of IT, we see the portfolios of existing and potential investments that crowd every corner of today's organisations, as plots of unworked land. A lot of people would rather not think too hard about the bacteria, worms and the organisms that populate those plots (Answer: hundreds of bacteria and up to a million fungi in every gram, as well as hundreds of worms, millipedes and other bugs!). To us, every organisation's IT environment is a hectare of uneven soil. But soil is an amazing thing. If appropriately planted, and with the right amount of water and sunlight and attention, amazing things can happen.

Aligning IT and the business

What does it mean to 'align IT and business'? What does it mean to 'add value to business' through IT? Indeed, what kind of 'value' are we talking about?

In practice, today there are three key focuses where businesses look to IT to deliver value:

- Improving operational business efficiency and effectiveness

- Managing risk and compliance

- Supporting innovation.

All these focuses actually place different emphases on 'value creation', but they all bring the same challenges – not least the need to effectively balance investment for the right mix of short-term and long-term paybacks. In reality, a business wants to drive towards all three of these things, and IT needs to be able to support all three in ways that fit with the mission in hand.

It's difficult to define an idea as broad as IT–business alignment succinctly, but a working definition should go something like this:

> *IT-business alignment is a collaborative process that businesspeople and IT organisations go through to create an environment in which investment in IT and delivery of IT services reflect business priorities, whether IT services are sourced internally or externally; and in which business priorities are influenced by understanding of IT capabilities and limitations.*

Aspects of IT–business alignment

The definition used above aims to highlight that there are three core aspects to IT–business alignment that must all be considered if things are to improve. The three aspects are three high-level phases of an overall IT lifecycle: investment, service delivery and change management.

Figure 1.2 shows these three aspects. First, let's look at the importance of considering IT investment. This reflects the fact that IT is now integral to the way that businesses operate. Historically, IT has been viewed by the business as somewhat of a 'black art', best left to IT practitioners, with the result that investment in IT has been treated as a special case. With IT now playing such a critical role, this position is no longer tenable. Investment in IT must be subject to the same priorities which govern investment in other assets – people, facilities, production lines, among others – on which the continued operation of the business depends.

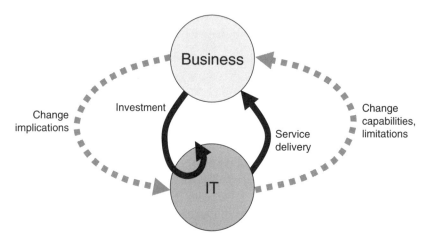

Figure 1.2: The elements of IT–business alignment

Second is the delivery aspect. This is a direct consequence of the first aspect. It highlights that the way in which the IT delivery organisation provides services to the business must be governed by the same business priorities. This extends to encompass the way that IT service delivery is measured. Only then will it be possible for businesspeople to assess the business return on their investment in IT.

Finally, with IT now so integral to the way that business operates, it is no longer feasible for business decisions to be taken without a clear understanding of the IT implications of those decisions. Business leaders and the IT delivery organisation must participate as peers in the business change management process and adopt a systematic approach to assessing the IT implications of any change. Such collaboration puts the IT organisation in a position where it can actually influence business change by highlighting the challenges and opportunities arising from technology change.

The principles of IT-business alignment

In our research, interviews and discussions, a number of core principles have emerged that are critical to bringing IT and business closer together. Before we list them, here's a serious caveat: to really make the most of IT in business, it's important to realise that both have to bend. Like two people locked in a small box, for an IT organisation and its business 'customer' to get comfortable, they both have to coordinate their actions so that neither gets an eye gouged or a foot stuck in an awkward place. Business and IT are intimately intertwined.

Either you decide to embrace the role of IT in business or you decide to ignore the possibilities and accept current state of compromise. If you're prepared to step up to the plate and take advantage of the benefits that modern IT and IT practices can bring to your organisation, you will have to be prepared for some discomfort. Recognise, however, that doing nothing and consigning your organisation to mediocrity is still a decision – unless, of course, you are already doing everything right – in which case we shall come to see you personally to present the champagne.

For the vast majority of organisations that wish to align their IT closer with the business, we believe there are a number of principles which, applied in the right way, will offer significant benefits over just sitting on hands and hoping some bright spark will take the problem away. We've condensed the findings of our research into six principles, and the later chapters will look at each one in more detail. These are as follows:

- *The IT organisation must get the basics right*: without the fundamentals of sound IT service delivery, it will be impossible to build the appropriate level of trust with the business.

- *Create a common language*: a shared understanding of goals, strategies, activities, metrics and change implications is a crucial foundation for the delivery of effective IT capabilities. A common language is essential for the establishment and maintenance of that shared understanding.

- *Establish a peer relationship between business and IT*: there needs to be real sharing of authority and responsibility when it comes to making and implementing decisions that have implications for business and IT.

- *Work towards coordinated goals and objectives*: a common language is not enough if ever-broadening communities of IT stakeholders are to be led in a way that promotes agreement on what's important and what isn't. IT–business alignment needs a culture that promotes working together in a coordinated way to meet shared goals and objectives.

- *Manage IT as a business-driven portfolio*: effective management of IT investments requires a big-picture view that does not just consider work that is planned or in progress, but also fully encompasses past investments to ensure a net overall contribution of value to the business from IT spending. This view needs to balance risks, costs and returns across the business as a whole.

- *Foster relationships with key IT suppliers*: effective supplier management is essential, because suppliers provide IT capabilities and are potentially an invaluable source of skills, resources and insights to help optimise the delivery and support of services to the business. More than that, though, a lack of supplier management can lead to higher costs, unnecessary risks and failure to maximise return on IT investments.

While these principles can be applied in isolation, there are many synergies and dependencies between them. If the IT organisation cannot establish business trust by getting the basics right, for example, then it becomes very difficult for IT to establish a peer relationship with the business. Similarly, coordinated goals and objectives can only be worked towards if there is a common language between business and IT.

A word about Enterprise Architecture

On a specific point, given that the central theme of this book is the alignment of IT activities with the business, and that this alignment must take place at all levels, it is worthwhile emphasising a thread that runs throughout our discussion that provides an important frame of reference.

You will find us using the term 'Enterprise Architecture' (EA) quite frequently, which is relatively common in IT industry parlance but can mean different things to different people. In the context of this book, we use EA to refer to that all-important framework for IT–business alignment.

At the highest level, EA is based on a mapping of organisational, process and IT structures and dependencies, and how these may need to change in the future to achieve business goals and objectives. We'll be discussing different perspectives on EA in context as we explore the various aspects of alignment activity, and particularly how the concept may be applied incrementally without running into 'analysis paralysis' and other problems which so often plague enterprise mapping and modelling exercises that attempt to 'boil the ocean'. So look out for references to EA as we go, as it is a crucial element in the overall equation.

Finding your way around this book

What does this book contain?

The book consists of four sections: a summary of where we are today and how we got here, the principles themselves, their application in a real-world environment and scorecards, as follows.

The current realities of business and IT

This section contains a brief overview of the history of IT and how things stand now: a complex interwoven network of business and IT challenges. The central question it poses is, given the 50 years of innovation we have seen, why is IT still not delivering business value? It then sets out the imperatives on IT–business alignment, defining what needs to be done to solve such challenges and to provide a firm foundation for future growth.

The principles

These sections describe the principles themselves. Each of the principles follows the same format:

- *Common areas of misalignment*: documents the issues faced by organisations today, to illustrate the need for the principle.

- *Alignment imperatives*: briefly defines where organisations need to get to and what that would look like.

- *Achieving alignment*: describes the core transformational advice and guidance and highlights the key actions to achieve alignment.

- *Maintaining alignment*: explains how to sustain alignment and prevent things drifting out of alignment over time.

- *Summary*: summarises the key challenges and actions.

For each principle, we explain the different stakeholders involved, their roles and their expectations. We also provide practical examples to show how the principles have been applied in the real world. The book does not shy away from investigating the tensions between the business and the IT department, as this understanding is key to overcoming the alignment impasse.

Applying the principles

This section maps out a path towards sustainable IT–business alignment, based on a series of four alignment goals – gain trust from the business, understand the business, engage the business and drive the business – through which the principles can be applied in a practical manner. It explains the role of Enterprise Architecture and outlines an agile approach to IT–business alignment to facilitate incremental application of the principles.

Scorecards

This section presents some practical checklists and questions to enable you to determine where you are in terms of the principles and their application. These are provided to help the business and the IT organisation gauge where they are along the evolutionary path towards alignment. Subsequently, the scorecards can be used as a basis for reviews and audits.

Who is it for?

This book provides practical guidance to business and IT professionals in technical and management roles in organisations that can benefit from improved IT–business alignment. While these organisations will tend to the larger (mainly because smaller companies can generally work around the challenges described here), we do not believe that the size of the organisation is the deciding factor; rather, it is dictated by the answers to such questions as

- Is IT currently constraining your organisation – are there business situations in which IT is a bottleneck?

- Is there a disconnect between how IT is deployed and operated, and what the business is trying to achieve?

- Has the potential of technology to be a differentiator thus far proved to be an elusive goal?

If this is the case, this book is for you. Its mission is to provide principles that any organisation can follow, at least in part, to derive tangible and direct benefit from their current and future IT investments.

We wrote this book to provide a common point of reference for IT and businesspeople. As such, it is written in plain English and does not descend into technical detail – though some terminology may be unfamiliar, it is clearly defined and explained. As such, the book provides a common vocabulary for both sides, to break through the mystique and jargon, and to lower the communication barriers between technical and nontechnical stakeholders.

Finally, the book is aimed at any other party with an interest in IT–business alignment, not least the IT supplier community. It explains how technology vendors, integrators and service providers should present their offerings to potential customers in a way that can maximise the chances of success.

2

The current realities of business and IT

We're now in the fifth decade since IT started to be used by mainstream private and public sector organisations. Given the 50 years of technical innovation that the IT industry has delivered, why is it that today, the value of organisations' IT investments is questioned more than ever?

The answer is twofold: the IT investments of yesterday have created both problems of technology complexity directly and business environments where the speed of change and the expectations of business executives are much greater than ever before. In other words, the positive outcomes of past IT investments have created new challenges, and the negative outcomes of those investments have made it difficult to meet those challenges.

The universal business challenges that have sprung from the power of IT to connect people and organisations around the world can't be stopped – that's 'progress'. It is possible to do something about overcoming the negative outcomes of past IT investments. But we can move forward only if we first understand how we got to where we are.

The true nature of IT

As we look around us at the way in which IT is deployed and used in organisations today, it is interesting to ponder how things ended up the way they are, particularly as it is extremely unlikely that we would see the same picture if organisations had the luxury of starting again with a clean sheet of paper. The sad truth is that no one in their right mind would actually design anything as complicated and convoluted as the average corporate IT landscape that exists today, with all the stresses, strains and challenges that come with it.

But this is the real world, and the fact of the matter is that IT capabilities and the way they are used and managed in any sizeable organisation have not come about according to some grand design, but through years of organic growth and evolution. And the word 'organic' here is a very important one. While IT may be thought of as predominantly an engineering-based discipline, when we look at its use holistically within a business environment, it has far more in common with the average garden than a well-oiled machine. An odd statement to make, perhaps, but one that acknowledges the reality of today's environment in which so many aspects of technology sometimes appear to have taken on a life of their own.

Time to start gardening?

The gardening analogy for IT management and evolution came about quite naturally as we were researching this book. The more we talked to IT strategists and leaders about their working environment, the more it sounded like a managed ecosystem made up of many individual components that coexist but if left to their own devices, would each evolve independently in their own natural way. The conclusion we came to was that just like the gardener, it's impossible for those running IT organisations to have absolute control. In a garden, for example, plants will always grow towards the sun and compete with each other for space, nourishment and light. Seeds will then drift in over the fence and take root, sometimes leading to a welcome addition to the garden, sometimes to weeds and nettles. Then there is unfavourable weather, pests and other inconveniences that every gardener, whether he likes it or not, has to live with.

The upshot is that gardens need to be managed, but in a way that takes account of these factors. And as anyone with a garden knows, this is an ongoing process – the job doesn't end when you have things looking just the way you want them. If left unmanaged, the behaviours and events we have discussed would lead a garden to degenerate into a mess. It's not that it wouldn't be full of healthy thriving plants, but the mix of those plants and the way in which they have grown would not necessarily meet our needs. In the same location, an ornamental garden and vegetable patch would end up looking pretty much the same if neglected for long enough.

And so it is with IT. In a world in which we are all surrounded by technology, in the high street and the home, as well as the workplace, there is no way to stop business users taking advantage of it. In many ways, it is therefore about managing which technology is used within the business and how, recognising that without such management, and on a continuous basis at that, things will rapidly degenerate into a mess just like in the garden. Along the way, it is necessary to deal with those things that influence how IT is used but which cannot be completely controlled:

- Human nature and organisational politics

- The business and economic environment

- The demands placed on IT by the business

- The increasingly complex technology landscape

- The relentless march of business expectation.

We explore these in more detail below, beginning with the human dimension, which is best illustrated through a quick political history of IT.

Human nature and organisational politics

In the beginning, was the mainframe...

Well, this is arguable depending on where you choose to start with your history lesson, but the point at which mainframes were the cornerstone of IT back in the 1970s is a convenient place to start when discussing the journey to today's computing environments. The key point is that mainstream computing began as a highly centralised activity that was heavily controlled by groups of specialist technicians upon whom the early users were completely dependent to serve their computing needs. This was not a problem then because the economics (i.e. expense) of computing meant that the use of systems was anyway restricted out of commercial necessity, in terms of both the number of employees who had access and the tasks to which systems were put, predominantly back-office number crunching type activity.

This situation was reflected in the politics and influence of early 'data processing' or DP departments as they were often called. Computer systems were regarded as something special, and those responsible for operating them generally had absolute authority over who could do what with the organisation's precious computing assets.

As time went on, however, a number of things happened to disrupt the *status quo*.

Branching out

The cost of computing began to fall as minicomputers were introduced and tools and techniques for software development matured and became more standardised. It is easy today to dismiss the programming languages of that time, such as COBOL and PL/1, as being clumsy and old fashioned, but they were key to allowing skill bases to be built up effectively in order to streamline the production and maintenance of the capability of the new business systems. The next obvious development was the emergence of 'software packages' – off-the-shelf solutions prebuilt to provide specific business functionality that could be bought, tailored and deployed much more quickly than the previous approach of developing software from scratch.

As a result of these developments, which in reality took place over a decade or so, the use of computing started to branch out across the business, with computers often even being deployed at departmental level to serve specific local needs in areas that would never have previously been able to justify access to the corporate mainframe. Through this more widespread use, however, something very important happened. Computers lost their 'special' status and started to become viewed as ordinary. Access to and use of 'the system' became a routine part of many people's jobs, and the more they used and relied on computers, the more they took them for granted and expected them to do what was required in the context of the business.

This represented the beginning of the rift between the IT organisation and the business it served, which is all too common today, because it was at about this time, in the early 1980s, that the user mindset shifted from accepting what they were given in computing terms to feeling that they had the right to demand what *they* required to do *their* jobs effectively. Initial frustration at being so dependent on a central IT organisation that didn't respond quickly enough when requests for new capabilities were made ultimately turned into a friction between the two camps, as disgruntled users stood in line and waited their turn to get what they wanted, often for months.

The innocent seed of anarchy

Against this background, it is no surprise in hindsight that when the personal computer (PC) came onto the scene, it was pounced on by many parts of the business, which saw it as a way to liberate themselves from the shackles of central IT. Then, as PC equipment, operating systems and packages evolved, and ultimately became networked, the personal and workgroup computing phenomenon just exploded, and try as they might, IT organisations could no longer retain the complete control they had become accustomed to.

Along the way, the introduction of client/server technology into the mix just aggravated the situation. Now, departments could procure and deploy comparatively cheap technology to run highly capable multiuser packages of their choice, with little involvement from central IT. Satellite IT groups began to spring up in many cases, as departments took it upon themselves to acquire the skills and resources necessary to manage their systems under the authority and budgetary control of line of business managers.

The anarchy, as some people would describe it, that ensued often drove an even bigger wedge between IT and the business, with the former now the frustrated party being unable to control what was deployed and how, yet still being expected to step in and bail out the anarchists when things went wrong. Meanwhile, the business often developed a view of the IT organisation as the 'productivity prevention department' – slow to act killjoys that didn't deliver what the business required but attempted to put constraints and blocks on the business when it attempted to solve its own IT problems.

Today, users are making unilateral decisions to use public internet services, mobile technology, personal productivity tools and so on, often again with the IT organisation two or three steps behind shouting 'What about security, privacy, compliance, backups, integration costs, maintenance costs, support overheads?' The users then come back and again question the IT organisation's ability to deliver what the business needs, highlighting the times when it apparently went off on its own agenda with Y2K, enterprise portals, dot-com distractions and obsessive lock-down security – and, of course, never keeping promises and spending too much money.

The current political reality

The current reality from a political perspective is that the IT organisation has often assumed the role of a servant, and an incompetent one at that, at least in the eyes of the business. This is probably the most frequent state of affairs we encounter in our research when we talk to businesspeople about their IT brethren: a mindset where the latter cannot be trusted to do what they are told and must be kept in line with harsh words and the occasional metaphorical beating.

The next most common state of affairs we encounter is where the IT powerbase has fought to keep its status and has set up in opposition to the business. Years of frustration and tension in these circumstances has led to what might best be described as an ongoing battle between IT and the business, with the two factions struggling to work together productively against a background of constant friction and conflict.

Neither of these two situations is conducive to effective IT–business alignment.

Of course, we also come across IT organisations that are working in relative harmony with the business, but even where this appears to be the case on the surface, you generally don't have to scratch too deeply to reveal at least some of the issues we have been discussing.

The bottom line is that, in the vast majority of cases, there is room for improvement in the way that the IT organisation and the business work together from a political and relationship perspective, and much of the subsequent advice in this book is designed to address this challenge either directly or indirectly.

Beyond this political reality, however, there is also a need to consider some of the realities of the external environment in which organisations operate.

The business and economic environment

The issues we have been discussing obviously haven't stopped the dramatic explosion in the use of technology for business purposes, to the point where IT is now pretty much woven into the fabric of the modern organisation and, indeed, into markets as a whole through the power of communication connections.

This has enabled people and organisations around the world to connect with each other and do business instantaneously, and has also created business environments where the speed of change and the expectations of business executives are much greater than ever before.

As a result, today's business and IT challenges are closely interwoven. Business challenges faced by organisations the world over have been significantly influenced by heavy investment in IT and communications. More and more, business networks and digital networks are indistinguishable from each other. Think about a typical financial institution or a telecommunications company, for example. What defines their businesses today? Mostly, it's the management of digital information. Money, phone calls, text messages – they're all just ones and zeros. But now think about a warehousing and distribution specialist, or a leading retail chain. How much is their business about understanding, managing and acting on digital information? These days, the answer is an awful lot.

Three universal, high-level business pressures

In our discussions with organisations, we find something curious when we ask executives about the pressures that are impacting them. Although retailers use different language to utilities, and public sector organisations use different language to financial services outfits, they all consistently refer to the impacts of three large-scale socio-economic forces: globalisation, transparency and smart, connected markets.

The forces of globalisation

Increasingly, global customer bases, partner networks, supplier networks and competition, enabled by the wide availability of instantaneous, global mass communications, are forcing organisations to become leaner and more flexible; to focus on what makes them different, giving everything else to others to look after; and to find new ways to connect with and deliver compelling value to their customers.

This frequently manifests itself in new, sophisticated approaches to technology and business process outsourcing, which are themselves enabled by that same global communications infrastructure. In this environment, business resources can feasibly be located anywhere: it is possible to consider that 'the world is flat' (as *New York Times* columnist Thomas Friedman explains in his book with the same name). This global availability of resources presents all organisations with significant opportunities for cost and other strategic advantages, as well as provides challenges to those operating in the private sector in the form of global competition.

The drive for transparency

Regulation is sometimes forced on organisations by governments, but increasingly they are also being forced by their customers and investors to provide more information about their processes, the resources they use and the ways in which they interact with their ecosystems and environments. And the drive for transparency isn't limited to the private sector: governments, too, are being pressurised by media and citizens to become much more open about how their machinery operates and the effects that they have on social and business communities.

The desire to engage effectively with smart, connected markets

The mass availability of high-speed, always-on communication connections is changing the ways in which consumers, citizens, suppliers, governments and markets interact, but this pressure isn't just about globalisation: it's about market expectations. Individuals and organisations are increasingly looking to the 'online world' for solutions to problems and opportunities before looking to the 'offline world', and spending much more time online – to work, play, share and collaborate.

Consumer behaviour and demand manifest themselves differently in this new environment, and private sector organisations are under pressure to connect with these evolved markets in the right ways. In the public sector, governments are keen to find new ways to engage citizens and businesses, and provide them with 'joined up' services.

Realities of the current business climate

When we consider these three forces, it is important to understand that we are not talking about a one time shift from the way business used to be done to some kind of new steady state. The effect of this shift on many organisations is to move them from a state of relative stability to an environment that is, almost by definition, in a constant state of flux. The combination of globalisation, transparency and increased connectedness means that individual participants, value chains and transaction mechanisms change in nature very quickly as new sets of circumstances arise. Indeed, many are driving their organisations forward by continuously and deliberately engineering new sets of circumstances designed to disrupt the *status quo*, create new opportunities and put the competition onto the back foot.

Of course, this shift has already largely taken place in markets such as financial services, although it is doubtful that anyone will escape its effects for much longer. The days of cosy, closed and stable marketplaces are pretty much over now and the dynamic global marketplace is here to stay.

Once of the consequences of this is to change the requirements for automation; so as organisations as a whole are flexing to operate in new ways at a business level, the world is changing for the IT organisations within them. The days of cosy, closed and stable long-term IT strategies are also over. If people today believe they can predict what needs to be in their IT landscapes in 5 years' time, they are in denial about how dynamic, interdependent and unpredictable the world is becoming.

Having said this, there are some specific directional shifts in the way in which the demands on IT are changing, which should be understood.

The demands placed on IT by the business

The business shifts discussed above are leading to a corresponding set of shifts in the focus of business automation.

Although IT was first used as a business tool to automate the storage, retrieval and analysis of structured data in the 'back office', organisations are now looking for ways to apply IT to increase the efficiency and effectiveness of the business processes which touch customers and partners, where the emphasis is on the automation of information exchange and collaboration between people and organisations.

As Figure 2.1 shows, yesterday's focus was on automating the aspects of stable, non-differentiating data management processes that are explicitly defined (such as accounting processes). In order to deal with the pressures of globalisation, transparency and engaging with smart, connected markets, today's focus for adding value from the use of IT has moved away from these 'back office', operational processes and towards automating aspects of differentiating processes that are more to do with how organisational management and strategy are coordinated. These processes are highly likely to be collaborative and dynamic in nature, span organisational boundaries and depend on tacit knowledge.

As IT organisations are being asked to support this shift in focus and enable organisations to open up to others, the business of 'doing' IT itself is changing in some profound ways:

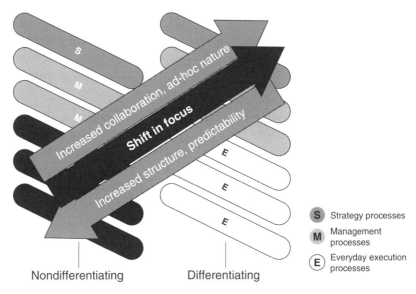

Figure 2.1: A profound shift in technology and effort focus

- The *focus of business automation* has moved from the back office to the 'front office' – where organisations interact with customers, partners and suppliers – and beyond (to emerging spaces where organisations collaborate with each other and with individual customers to drive innovation, for example).

- The *personal computing environments* that individuals interact directly with on their desks (or on their laps) have changed considerably in scope. In the past, most workers with access to a personal computer of some kind worked primarily with personal productivity tools and business application user interfaces – all of which presented tightly bound domains of interactivity and functionality. Now, however, a great many workers have their desktops augmented with instantaneous access to a global network of information and business resources – the Web.

- The focus of *technology innovation* has shifted from effective storage and processing of structured data to various applications of information communication. Now the real focus of IT innovation is on supporting various types of collaboration scenario and the effective integration of heterogeneous and widely distributed systems and information sources.

- Decisions within organisations about the *supply of IT-related capabilities* have become more sophisticated, enabled by the globalisation of IT skills and high-speed global communications networks. Although historically outsourcing (or insourcing) was carried out at a relatively coarse-grained level – with responsibility for procuring and managing large chunks of IT infrastructure and applications being sourced in the same way – now organisations are starting to make much more selective and granular decisions about how IT capabilities are sourced. Software-as-a-service (SaaS), managed infrastructure services, business process outsourcing, offshore application development, 'open source' software tools – all these are variations on capability sourcing options, and increasingly organisations are looking to pursue multiple options simultaneously.

- The nature of IT *project implementation* has changed significantly, too. The big decision used to be 'buy versus build'. Now, it's a truism that 'all development is integration, and all integration is development'. In many organisations, the initial deployment of technology to automate the key aspects of business is over. Applications may not currently be delivered in the right form and in the right place, but the functionality is there somewhere. Now the focus is on how to make things work better, so projects typically involve mixtures of off-the-shelf application procurement, software development and integration. With the shift to service-oriented architecture (SOA) and SaaS models, many organisations are starting to add capability rental to the project input mix. Figure 2.2. summarises these.

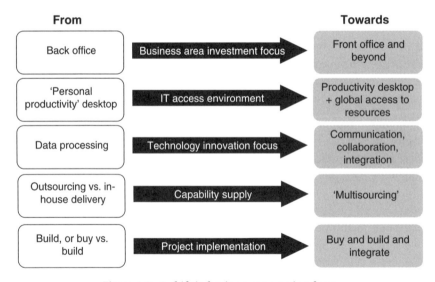

Figure 2.2: A shift in business automation focus

Realities of adjusting to changing demand

A crucially important consequence of all these changes is that in order to deliver real value in meeting today's underlying business needs and responding to business pressures, the canvases on which IT organisations create business solutions have to broaden radically.

Although IT organisations used to be able to satisfy their business masters by focusing purely on addressing the specific business requirements arising at any one time, now they have to do more. While keeping the required outcome from immediate needs in mind, they have to consistently ask themselves: 'are we also working to help the organisation as a whole be more effective?' The scope of IT concern has shifted from solving point problems within organisations to improving entire ecosystems.

The increasingly complex technology landscape

Although many industries enforced a 'pause for reflection' on IT investment a few years back during the economic downturn, technology innovation has continued unabated. New devices are added to the mix all the time: mobile phones can access the Internet, and indeed, computers can be used as phones. Software development has taken the client–server model to its logical conclusion, in the shape of SOA – where any software component can interact with any other, anywhere. Today organisations are learning about web services and mashups, blogging and wireless networks. IT is once again getting exciting. But many organisations still suffer from the same old problems and indeed have to support the same old systems that date right back to the earliest days. Our research suggests that over 75% of all computer systems are based on technologies and designs that are considered as 'legacy'.

The problem is that in the world of IT, very little ever dies. Despite the bold predictions from pundits, the systems built during a previous wave of innovation are rarely completely replaced by capabilities delivered in the next. The population of mainframe technology suppliers may have dwindled significantly over the past 10–15 years, but IBM is still experiencing growth in mainframe shipments of MIPs (millions of instructions per second) capacity.

In a 2006 Arcati Research survey, nearly 90% of large users of mainframes (using 10 000+ MIPS) said they were growing their mainframe capacity by 10–25%. In discussions of IBM's Q3 '06 financial results, CFO Mark Loughridge announced that the installed base of IBM mainframe capacity had grown past 10 million MIPS for the first time in IBM's history.

Complexity in multiple dimensions

This steady accretion of infrastructure and functionality over time has made individual systems much more complex. More and more, the priority is to build IT capabilities that cut across organisational departments to align with important end-to-end business processes, and more often than not this means building bridges between multiple different, and distributed, hardware and software platforms in order to orchestrate functions across multiple existing systems. With technology like Enterprise Application Integration (EAI) and new approaches like SOA, the construction of these multifaceted systems is much more manageable. But coordinating the work required to optimise them, uncover faults and fix them is still a tough problem. IT organisations tend to be arranged into specialised teams, each of which focuses on administering a particular type of technology environment using its own administration tools and approaches.

The question of control and ownership

This cross-organisational bridging also has repercussions in terms of the stakeholders in IT project delivery because invariably the capabilities which need to be joined together are influenced, if not controlled, by different business groups, each with their own agendas and priorities. This makes it difficult to get agreements to allow the bridges to be built and also raises the uncomfortable question of who owns the bridges once they're in place.

Ownership of and accountability for these complex IT capabilities is further complicated by the increasingly sophisticated approaches that organisations are taking to sourcing particular IT and business capabilities, and the increasing degree of interconnection between organisations and their customers, partners and suppliers. Figure 2.3. illustrates the resulting picture.

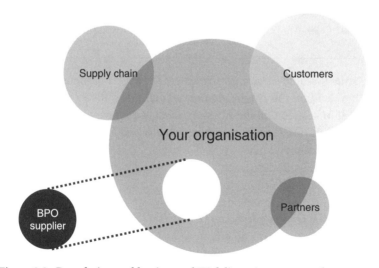

Figure 2.3: Boundaries are blurring, and IT delivery is more complex as a result

More and more, IT organisations are finding that in order to deliver high-level IT capabilities, they have to work with resources that might have been built in-house, but which are now managed externally; resources that are delivered over the Internet and rented on a monthly basis; resources that are owned and managed by customers, partners and suppliers; and more.

Technology landscape realities

The reality is that in many of today's IT organisations, the existing technology landscape – and the services and teams that work to deliver capabilities from that technology – tend to be organised to avoid or withstand change, rather than to work with it. Moreover, human psychology resists change and likes control. Both of these characteristics work against any attempts to improve how IT capabilities are delivered. People (both businesspeople and IT people) naturally want control, not alignment and cooperation.

This challenge is particularly complicated to overcome because as organisations become more interlinked, their IT landscapes become more integrated and IT sourcing becomes more sophisticated; the truth is that there are going to be multiple IT domains which influence the way that business gets done in your organisation – and not all of them will be under your control.

The relentless march of business expectation

After decades of IT investment and decades of penetration of IT into the lives of consumers, expectations of IT – and of IT organisations – within organisations are generally much higher than ever before.

First of all, it's clear from our research that those decades of IT investment have created a level of 'saturation' of IT within business that has given business executives a much greater awareness of how IT (and the business capabilities that it supports) affects organisations' performance. This is driving a much greater level of maturity in organisations' understanding and treatment of IT as an investment category, leading to IT investment being considered just like any other big investment. IT is seen as a business tool, and significant capital investments in IT are increasingly subjected to the same controls and oversight as significant capital investments in new offices or factories.

IT budgets are tightly managed today as a consequence of this greater understanding. These days, executive boards are no more likely to sanction the kinds of double-digit year-over-year percentage IT budget growths that were seen in the 1990s, than they are to sanction similar growth in expenditure on facilities.

Furthermore, IT, and technology, in general, is now available everywhere and is accessible to everyone. In the United Kingdom, for example, a 'pay as you go' mobile phone costs only tens of pounds, and a laptop computer can be purchased for only a few hundreds. There are two significant outcomes of this greater awareness of technology that surface in the business environment:

- There is very little to stop the average Joe user from buying technology using discretionary budgets in order to get a job done and avoiding what they see as 'jumping through corporate hoops'. This is simply a continuation of the psychology that emerged two decades ago around the personal computer, but with the commoditisation of even very sophisticated technologies, the challenge of managing this behaviour is much more acute today.

- There is much greater awareness within employee populations of what IT can and should be able to do. We've had numerous conversations with business executives, which contain variations on the following lament: 'when I'm at home and I want to find the answer to a question, I go to Google and get an answer, from a website in Malaysia, within seconds. When I'm at work and I need to know a particular detail of the current sales situation in my territory, I have to cajole the IT department, which is just down the corridor, and at best I have to wait a day'.

User expectation realities

Gone are the days when the IT organisations could use their technical insights and know how to claim the high ground when discussing technology and requirements for its use with users. Individuals in business today are both IT savvy and empowered to solve their own problems. The trouble is that although they are able to move forward under their own steam, in many cases they are totally unaware of the dangers and consequences of their actions. Issues such as security, privacy, compliance and cost effectiveness are not necessarily part of the equation as they make their own technology choices. Sometimes this is not an issue, but often it is, so an IT organisation that is not fulfilling expectations can easily find itself in greater difficulties as it is burdened by the distraction of having to assume responsibility for something which it cannot directly control.

This brings us right back to where we started: the concept of the technology garden.

Adopting a realistic approach

Against the backdrop of these realities, it is important to move forward with an equally realistic mindset and approach.

You can no more change human nature than a gardener can change the tendency for shoots to grow up and roots to grow down. Neither can you control the business environment, the evolution of new technologies and the emergence of ideas in the broader IT industry, and many of the other things we have discussed.

On occasions, you may be able to assert your will in the same way that a gardener prunes a tree, cuts back a shrub or removes an unwanted weed, but push things too far and permanent damage can occur, disrupting the overall balance of the garden. Cultivating, nurturing, coaxing and encouraging are therefore equally important techniques to shape things in the way you want and to either keep them that way or reshape them in a managed way over time. Just as the most successful gardeners work *with* natural tendencies rather than against them, the most successful IT organisations do the same with individual IT users, business management, technologies and suppliers.

In the principles that follow, we provide specific advice and guidance on how to cultivate this kind of approach to achieve sustainable alignment of business and IT, beginning with a review of some of the basics that need to be in place before you can move forward. After all, you wouldn't start gardening without a good water supply, adequately nourished soil and understanding of what's already planted!

3

The IT organisation must get the basics right

It organisations want to build more strategic relationships with business heads, but it's not realistic to do that if IT can't meet basic expectations. Trust is the key to any relationship, and there are a number of reasons why trust has been lacking – not least, disappointing IT systems, poorly-executed projects, and a lack of responsiveness from IT organisations. While 'get the basics right' sounds easy, things are rarely that simple. A sound starting point is to focus your energy on delivering services to business users, rather than managing technology components. A services-based approach provides a stimulus for reviewing existing IT capabilities and their costs. Armed with that information, you can work on the processes and skills required for consistent IT service delivery. The work you do which leads to this understanding demands meaningful engagement with business teams, drives dialogue, and makes trust easier to build.

Common areas of misalignment

> '*IT was a black art – and it still is to some extent.*'
>
> Dale Nix of consultancy Chapman-Nix,
> previously Sales Planning Director at Forté Hotels

As we have already discussed, the last 50 years of IT investment have resulted in an environment where business and technology are intimately intertwined. Business success is increasingly dependent on the exploitation of digital information and automated support of business activities. However, far from creating an environment where the relationship between business and IT prospers, the result is a clash of heightened business expectations and technical complexity. IT sometimes astounds, but more often disappoints leading to a lack of trust.

Trust is at the heart of any intimate relationship, and the relationship between IT and business is no different. Unless businesspeople are able to trust the IT environment and the organisation which provides it, the IT–business alignment is always going to be challenging. There are a number of common complaints from the business side which are indicative of this lack of trust: the most fundamental is the fact that IT fails to deliver on its promises.

IT systems simply do not work as expected . . .

The basic capabilities offered by IT should just work. For many in the organisation, these basic capabilities are office automation applications and business support systems, together with e-mail and Internet access. Straightforward enough – but for a variety of reasons they often fail to meet business expectations of functionality, availability, performance and usability. If e-mail grinds to a snail's pace at certain times of the day and core systems that support sales, service and operations are frequently unavailable because of failures or the need for maintenance, then it is no wonder that the IT organisation's reputation is so often called into question and trust is lacking. The unfortunate reality is that, as shown in Figure 3.1 below, IT capabilities frequently miss the target, both in terms of the initial promise and the agreed requirement.

The oft-heard retort of the IT department that it is unrealistic to expect every IT system, application and service to run continuously without a hitch is not an acceptable defence. It *is* realistic for the business to expect a certain level of basic functionality and service. To aggravate the situation, increasing levels of automation in the home have raised

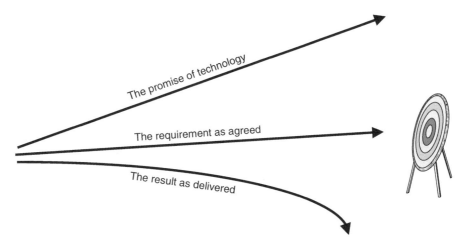

Figure 3.1: IT capabilities fail to hit the target on promised and agreed expectations

expectations across the board, such that IT capabilities at work seem even more unsatisfactory. What once may have been perceived as an acceptable level of service can quickly pale when computers used in the home are more capable, reliable and better connected than those available in the office.

The IT organisation may want a more strategic conversation with the business, but is this realistic if the fundamentals are not in place and working? Not according to Malcolm Whitehouse, IS Director and CIO in the UK Government's Department of Work and Pensions (DWP):

'Why should I talk to you about strategy if you can't make my PC work every day? For IT to move from being perceived as a cost and a necessary evil to a business enabler of value, IT needs to demonstrate that what IT already does is delivering value. If the business sees that their desktop is not working or that the network is failing then they are not going to perceive that IT is delivering value now let alone in the future.'

This view is echoed by Andreas Dietrich, CIO of SBB:

'Many CIOs and IT managers are still struggling with their infrastructure. Before business units can accept you as a partner, you have to show that you manage your basics correctly – infrastructure must run, and applications must work; service level agreements must be in place and must be met.'

Andreas' last point about service level agreements (SLAs) is well made, as they are primarily about agreeing and meeting the expectations of the business. Thus when IT fails to meet agreed service levels, the business rightly draws the conclusions that there may be a lack of operational rigour within the black box that is the IT organisation and that IT is simply not up to scratch.

... *and when there are problems they can be difficult to resolve*

All too frequently, when things do go wrong, they are difficult to put right. Or at least, that is the perception of the business: the elapsed time between a problem being logged with the help desk and achieving a resolution can lead to that conclusion. Indeed, it is not always apparent that the fault is being treated at all because of a lack of feedback on the progress of the IT organisation. The result is yet more disappointment, as John Johnson, CIO at Intel points out:

> *'Many of the problems in Intel IT in the past were to do with not meeting user expectations. Truthfully, at that point in time [7 years ago], we were operationally weak yet were not acknowledging this weakness when making promises.'*

When information is forthcoming, it is often not presented in terms that the business understands. A typical employee will be most interested in the resumption of service and not whether a certain patch has been applied or a firewall has been reconfigured. As shown in Figure 3.2, a focus on individual technologies, rather than on what technology enables,

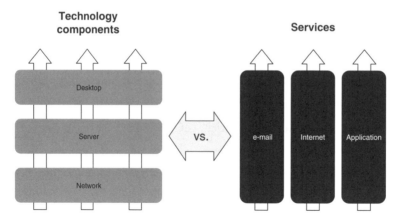

Figure 3.2: There is a tendency to focus on technology components rather than the services they enable

results in a kind of myopia: problems are often discussed in terms of servers, networks and software rather than services experienced by the business. This also results in a failure to prioritise effectively – there's always plenty to be done – with the result that the IT organisation comes across as reactive and flustered, rather than proactive and in control.

This tendency to focus on component technologies rather than business-facing services also results in failures to allocate responsibility and accountability. 'That's a network problem', says one technician; 'No, it's a database problem', says another. The consequence can be finger pointing: while stories of locking diverse groups of technicians into a room until they resolve a problem may be apocryphal, they are uncomfortably believable.

The recurrence of particular faults and the creation of workarounds by the IT organisation are just two common symptoms of a reactive, rather than proactive, approach to problem resolution. If fire fighting is the norm, there can be little time for fire prevention with the result that in many organisations, the potential for preventative maintenance or pre-emptive actions to free up resources, as shown in Figure 3.3, is no more than a distant hope.

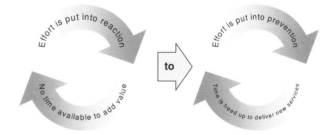

Figure 3.3: A proactive approach to problem resolution frees up resources for new capabilities

Inability to respond effectively to requests from the business ...

Even when there are no faults, the IT organisation struggles to respond to requests from the business. These can range from the simplest of requirements, for example, a password reset or a file restore from backup, through to the implementation of new applications or the definition of new IT requirements. As a result, complaints from the business that the IT organisation simply doesn't understand what it needs are all too common.

Part of the problem is the technology-centric view discussed above. Rather than focusing first on what the business is trying to achieve – 'better team working' or 'improved collaboration' – the IT organisation too often starts with available technologies and tries to fit business needs to the capabilities they provide. However, we can't lay all the blame for a "technology first" view at the IT organisation's door. It's frequently the case that businesspeople are convinced by their peers in industry of the power of a given solution or piece of kit and use their buying power to bring it into the organisation without any IT oversight.

As we discuss in Chapter 4, while such attitudes prevail and in the absence of a shared understanding of technology capabilities, it is difficult to reach an agreement when it comes to new IT requirements or changes in existing systems. These challenges are compounded by the fact that the processes in place to support the implementation of changes or new requirements are often a bottleneck. Simple requirements are lost in the machine or hidden under layers of bureaucracy, while sponsors of more sophisticated requirements are forced to jump through hoops of business cases, authorisations and value assessments.

. . . and projects typically do not meet expectations

Even once the projects have been funded and authorised, they may be subjected to delays and other problems, as complexity and chaotic management processes conspire to limit the chances of success. It is a frequently quoted statistic that most IT projects end in failure:

> *According to a 2004 Standish Group study,[1] whilst success rates in US IT projects were improving, no more than a third of all projects were deemed 'successful'. The remainder were either 'challenged' – that is , running late, over budget and/or lacking critical features – or, in 15% of the cases, had failed to deliver at all.*

Even when successful, by the time some IT projects are completed, the world has moved on, rendering requirements obsolete or downright wrong: for example, a networking security project that fails to take into account the security issues of wireless networks. Requirements may change for very good reasons, but little extra funding is available for changes and improvements beyond the initial business case. In any case, the will to make changes rarely lasts beyond the end of a project, says Darin Brumby, CIO at First Group:

> *'So finally when you've built something, you say, "There it is, there's the ERP [Enterprise Resource Planning] platform, we're finally there," then everyone breathes a sigh of relief, and forgets it. It is legacy from day one because we're not going to touch that platform now: it took us four years to do, so we're not touching it for another four years.'*

---

[1] 10th edition of the annual CHAOS report from the Standish Group (http://www.softwaremag.com/ L.cfm?Doc=newsletter/2004-01-15/Standish)

Business cannot see the value of IT

The final complaint we hear in our research is that the business struggles to understand what the IT organisation is up to and how it delivers value, which can only serve to exacerbate the difficulties discussed above. Fundamentally, this is symptomatic of reporting problems at multiple levels.

Few IT organisations have a comprehensive understanding of the IT environment, let alone what it costs and how it is used. Furthermore, they struggle to monitor the status of IT systems that are typically widely distributed throughout the organisation.

Reporting, where it happens, is not always presented in a way that makes sense to the business. It is one thing to report on the number of desktops or service calls; it is quite another, as we discuss in Chapter 4, to do so in a way which shows how much of a difference IT is making by linking information about the operational performance of IT investments to business-meaningful metrics. As a result it can be difficult for business-people to grasp the real value of IT or to prioritise IT investments: spending becomes a case of doing what is unavoidable, rather than what is necessary for the business.

Alignment imperatives

A common theme which permeates the preceding discussion is that a focus on specific technologies, rather than the services they enable, leads to misalignment. Key to resolving the issues, then, is a focus on service delivery.

Services, as we discuss elsewhere, are a way of talking about IT capabilities that is understandable to businesspeople, so a focus on service delivery provides a framework for a more effective relationship between IT and the business. Services in the real world are experienced through agreements between suppliers and customers rather than through intimate customer knowledge of implementation, and IT services should be no different. They should be presented in the context of customer expectations, costs and appropriate support mechanisms. With the right focus, the result is transparency: IT delivers against realistic and costed expectations; business and IT work together on the basis of what is achievable rather than what is desired, increasing the chances that expectations might actually be met. It's vital to remember that a service is something you experience, not something you build (proponents of Service Oriented Architecture should bear this in mind). A service-based approach to IT delivery, therefore, has to encompass the whole lifecycle of a service together with the processes which support the development, deployment and operation of its implementation – in contrast to the fragmented approach that is common in many organisations today.

An approach based on services provides a solid foundation for IT–business alignment because it focuses on meeting expectations in a way that the business understands and so establishes trust. It also frees up resources to help the IT organisation break out of the reactive approach and, as we discuss in later principles, make further improvements to service delivery provided to the business.

Achieving alignment

Review the current IT environment against service expectations

To get the house in order, the first step is to understand the relationship between the capabilities that IT is currently providing to the business and the business expectations of those capabilities. This is obviously necessary to establish what is out there; but equally, if not more, important is that it serves to open a dialogue and involve the business from the very start.

Although it might be possible to conduct a comprehensive review of absolutely everything in the IT environment across all lines of business, this is neither desirable nor necessary. What is most important is to identify those capabilities that the business itself sees as critical and also to look for areas of IT that are considered to be particularly weak. These areas can be elicited from the business using a number of techniques such as user surveys, group discussions and management reviews.

Using these as a starting point, you should be prepared to take a clipboard, sit down with individuals in the lines of business and find out the answers to such questions as:

- What services are they using? It is important to get the business perspective on this (Example: 'I use the sales tracking service'), but given the historical focus on technology components rather than services being delivered, do not be surprised if individuals refer to 'systems' or 'databases.'

- What are the expectations on each service? For example, are any activities seen as business critical, and what impact does this have for service delivery (Example: 'I couldn't do without e-mail on Friday, that's when we send out the supplier reports'.)

- Are particular services unsatisfactory, and are there any problems which have a negative business impact? (Example: 'The colour printer hasn't worked for 2 weeks, so we haven't been able to send out brochures'.)

- What is the status of each service in terms of project delivery? (Example: 'The quality of customer data is poor and we were promised an upgrade 2 months ago'.)

- How is the IT department perceived in terms of each service? (Example: 'Generally when there's a problem with the software somebody comes to fix it straight away, but if it's hardware, you have to wait a week'.)

- Are there dependencies between services? (Example: 'If there are problems with inventory management then we can't process orders fast enough'.)

- Are there opportunities for service improvement? (Example: 'If the sales system was down every Tuesday evening rather than Saturday evenings that would be great, because it's the busiest time for online orders'.)

It is important to focus on those services that are considered 'core': these are the ones the business cannot do without to support its day-to-day activities. Achieving a consistent level of information is very important – one person's critical system will be unimportant to others, so be prepared to analyse the results, revisit areas that are unclear and broker an agreement between different lines of business.

The result of the exercise is a high-level picture of business expectations of the services it deems critical, how well those expectations are being met and the priority services to focus on. You should be prepared to present the results back to the business, for review and feedback. While the results may be disappointing in some cases, this serves to further the dialogue; also, quite frankly, it leaves the IT organisation with no place to hide. Once the priority services have been identified and agreed, there will be little excuse for not treating them.

Build a picture of the cost of IT

Do you know how much it costs to deliver the services that you provide? This is not always apparent, says Darin Brumby, CIO at First Group:

'When we were embarking on the journey, the main focus was on 'the number', how much the company was spending in IT, but we didn't know "the number". The board was saying, "You must be spending circa 25 million in IT" So, I said, "That is what I expect my technicians to say, 'circa.' You guys should know. If you don't, we've got bigger problems than you think". When we worked out "the number" the reality was, it was much larger. The operational budget was 50 million, and we were potentially spending upwards of 100 million in capital, on projects underpinned by IT.'

Getting a handle on costs is an essential prerequisite for aligning IT with the business. Not only does it raise the level of dialogue between the two sides, but it also provides a basis on which the business is able to assess the value of IT. It is vital to build a picture of costs that are clearly attributable to IT service delivery, explains Angela Yochem, a senior executive at one of the United States' largest banking organizations:

'If you're trying to talk to the business you have to know the soft costs as well as the hard costs of what you do – and to be able to apply this knowledge to potential decisions.'

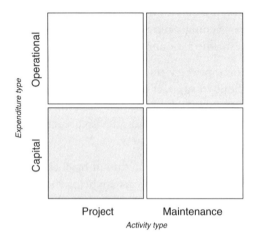

Figure 3.4: The dimensions of IT cost relate to type of expenditure and type of activity

To understand the true cost of service delivery, it helps to have a high level analytical framework in place. Figure 3.4 shows our framework, which highlights four areas where costs are incurred in IT service delivery. There are two dimensions of cost:

- Type of expenditure: capital versus operational

- Type of activity: project versus maintenance.

You should use the above model to help you uncover hidden costs and associate them with IT services. This may require an amount of detective work, particularly when IT procurement and management is spread across the lines of business. The kinds of costs you should look for include

- Project activity: capital expenditure: software licenses; infrastructure hardware; among others.

- Project activity: operational expenditure: staff costs from analysts, programmers, testers, project managers and other stakeholders (business representatives); among others.

- Maintenance activity: capital expenditure: additional software licenses; replacement parts; software upgrade licenses; among others.

- Maintenance activity: operational expenditure: floorspace rental; facilities/utilities spending; administration staff costs; among others.

As we mention a number of times throughout this book, sustained service delivery from IT organisations means bridging the gap that exists between project-focused teams and maintenance/administration teams. As we discussed earlier, services are experienced and demand consideration of the service lifecycle. Both teams are therefore involved in service delivery, and links must be established between them if a service-oriented approach is going to yield results. It's the same when it comes to analysing the cost of delivering a service: you have to consider both project and maintenance costs. Equally, it is important to recognise that some operational costs are difficult to allocate to specific IT services and may be managed by different parts of the organisation, so they have often been ignored: power is one such example.

Although it will not be possible to calculate the exact costs of IT service delivery, it is important nonetheless to get a picture of the scale of those costs to provide a basis for dialogue. Along with functionality and operational quality, a framework that incorporates the costs associated with service delivery provides a foundation for establishing a commercial relationship between IT and the business. You can't deliver a real service if the commercial aspects of delivery are left as an exercise for the consumer: that's a key part of how many IT organisations got into the mess they're in.

Define and implement a base set of procedures

Just as costs appear in four areas in the delivery of services (see Figure 3.4 above), so do many of the risks to service delivery. Operational best practice exists to assure that levels of service delivery are maintained: what's surprising is that the state of best practice in many organisations – and in the IT industry which serves them – is only just starting to wake up to the different areas, never mind how to minimise risks across the entire service life cycle.

When considering service delivery risks, it's traditional to focus on operational costs across project and maintenance activities. For project activities, development and management methodologies such as PRINCE2 (Projects in a Controlled Environment) and Dynamic Systems Development Methodology (DSDM) can help you get control of operational resource overruns and ensure that you deliver capabilities on time and within budget (in an ideal world). Likewise in the operational maintenance sphere, the Information Technology Infrastructure Library (ITIL) currently reigns supreme, with many large organisations on the path to implementing ITIL recommendations reporting significant improvements in their performance in the ongoing service delivery.

But what of the risks associated with capital expenditure in the execution of project and maintenance activities? Frameworks such as PRINCE2 and ITIL focus on getting people to work effectively on problems; they don't consider the risks associated with poor outcomes from capital investment decisions. Control Objectives for Information and Related Technology (COBIT) version 4's 'Plan & Organise' and 'Acquire & Implement' processes do focus to some degree on the importance of making sound capital investment decisions, but there is little focus available in the realm of 'industry standard' methods.

In Chapter 9 we discuss the role of enterprise architecture and architects to deal with this set of risks and challenges, and in Chapter 8, the importance of a strong IT supplier management capability. Very often though, organisations focus to a disproportionate degree on mature industry methods and fail to consider practices to address other risks. You need to make sure that you take a balanced and broad view if you're serious about a service-oriented view of IT to help you get the basics right.

There is no one-size-fits-all standard methodology for end-to-end service delivery; but at the same time, neither does every part of a framework or methodology have to be applied for it to be useful. A good starting point to know what best practices should be implemented is the output from the initial review work against service expectations. It may be that projects are failing to deliver, for example, or that service requests are taking too long to process. Depending on what is going wrong, you should evaluate the relevant off-the-shelf process frameworks and deploy the appropriate resources, training and potentially, the automation tools to plug the gaps in your existing processes. The key is to be pragmatic and take things one step at a time. Explains Darin Brumby, CIO at First Group:

> '*If anyone tells me they're doing ITIL completely inside their organisation, I say, really? Just give me a couple of those 32 processes, how about some incident reporting and some change management, that would be good for starters. We put in a basic, simplified version of PRINCE2, but tied to the governance model of the organisation. Basically what we're saying is, pick any model and then contextualise it for the sector that you're working in.*'

Transformation of operational service delivery processes such as the ones Darin mentions above – incident reporting and change management – are likely to require co-ordination with executives from lines of business, who may traditionally have 'responsibility' for some specific capabilities or processes. Regardless of what makes sense in terms of detailed process ownership, the IT organisation does need a clear overall picture of the issues across the IT environment. This is as true for ongoing projects in development, as service delivery post-deployment: we discuss this coordination role in greater detail in Chapter 5, where we introduce 'service managers' who are responsible and accountable for the delivery of services to the business.

Define service contracts

The understanding of existing systems and services outlined above, together with the expectations that the business has for them, provides the basis for the definition of achievable service levels that can be agreed with the business. Just as contracts apply between service providers and consumers in the real world, so should such agreements be in place between business and IT – although without all of the legal baggage.

The components of a service contract incorporate elements of standard SLAs, including the following, which primarily focus on the quality of the service:

- Availability: the times that each service must be accessible and to what level. For example, some services may be required '24 by 7', whilst others may be required '8 by 5'.

- Performance: the responsiveness of services in terms of time taken and in terms of ability to support multiple individuals.

- Fault management: the mechanisms invoked and time taken to correct a fault, or to resume service in the event of failure.

Service contracts should also be specified in terms of the functionality provided – the 'what' – and the cost of service delivery – the 'how much' – in addition to 'how well' the service is performed, which is the traditional focus of IT-focused service level agreements.

The primary objective is to balance the expectations of the business with a realistic view of what is achievable. This will require negotiation, involving some tough decisions and compromises, and the business will not be completely satisfied with all of the outcomes. It is therefore important to highlight the cost and resource implications of yielding to all of their demands. This gap between expectations and what is achievable is important because it provides an opportunity to prioritise future investments to close the gap where the business deems it appropriate.

Nor will it be possible to address all of the services at once at this stage, so it is most important to focus on a foundation of stable services that the business has agreed is most critical and then build on that foundation over time. Service contracts should be both appropriate and achievable, otherwise there is no point in having them: once the IT organisation signs up to a service contract, it must adhere to it, otherwise business will not trust any future plans. Explains Malcolm Whitehouse, IS Director and CIO in the UK Government's Department of Work and Pensions (DWP):

'There is a quality threshold for what IT does today. You need to demonstrate the quality of today's capabilities and that the plans to improve those capabilities are robust. If the business is to put more eggs into the IT basket, then business needs to be absolutely convinced that IT is capable of supporting them, so today's services must be resilient and robust.'

The discussion also extends to existing and prospective suppliers. In Chapter 8 we discuss the crucial role that supplier management plays in IT service delivery. The establishment of service levels discussed above will highlight dependencies on capabilities provided by suppliers and so they should be included in discussions, as Malcolm Whitehouse, IS Director and CIO in the UK Government's Department of Work and Pensions (DWP) points out:

> '*Entry-level criteria apply to service management and project delivery. These entry-level criteria must also be explained to supplier community as well as the business and the suppliers must buy into it too.*'

Start delivering

For all these efforts, it will be difficult to engage with the business in a meaningful way if conversations are still monopolised by problems in the existing environment. To take the conversation to the next level, it is first necessary to deal with such baggage. Darin Brumby, CIO at First Group, emphasises this point:

> '*When there's heaps to do strategically with IT, but the helpdesk doesn't work, eventually you just get sick of having every conversation with somebody saying, "But, I can't get through to the Help Desk". So first, you have to fix the helpdesk; then, you can say, "Right, can we now have a dialogue at the next level please? The helpdesk is fixed now".*'

A number of issues will have been flushed out in the review process, as will a number of opportunities to deal with issues simply and cost-effectively, in a way that directly benefits the business and demonstrates that the IT organisation is responsive to business needs. These and other opportunities for 'quick wins' can help deliver early value and build a level of trust.

However, that is only the start, and it is important to start tackling some of the bigger issues. Clearly, challenges relating to business-critical services should take priority and should be fed into project and service delivery processes to ensure that they are treated appropriately.

Maintaining alignment

Continuous improvement

Having developed an understanding of the IT environment, in terms of the IT services provided to the business and the technologies they depend on, and having put in place the processes to ensure that service delivery expectations are met and trust established, it is important to recognise that ongoing business and technology changes will erode the value of that investment, as shown in Figure 3.5 below.

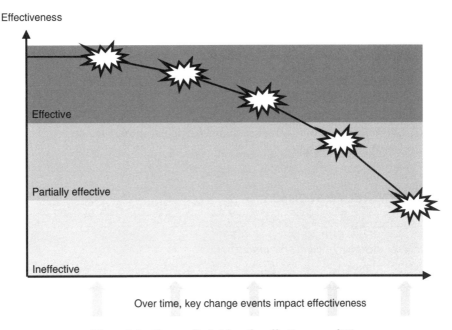

Figure 3.5: Change diminishes the effectiveness of IT

A process of ongoing audit and review, in line with effective quality management practices, is essential to counter this erosion. In particular, the following should be subjected to regular review:

- The core set of IT services and business expectations, and how well those expectations are being met

- The effectiveness of operational procedures

- The costs of the existing IT environment

- The delivery status of IT projects

- The skills and capabilities of the IT organisation.

Not only does a review process serve to stave off the descent into chaos, but it also provides the foundation for improvement: to extend the scope of core services, enhance the overall effectiveness of IT, and consequently increase the level of business trust. The audit process should extend to all of those responsible for IT service delivery, including external suppliers and, where core services are their responsibility, the lines of business.

One approach which our research has shown to be very effective, particularly to ensure that the review process is inclusive, is to train IT staff to undertake reviews on each other. Senior IT management must ensure that this is positioned correctly, with an emphasis on collaboration to enhance the business perception of the IT organisation rather than to highlight weaknesses within the IT organisation. When undertaken correctly, such reviews can be brisk affairs, the output consisting of a small set of achievable priorities, together with realistic timescales for action.

Reviews should be a regular feature of the *modus operandi* of the IT organisation, with the resulting actions feeding into the ongoing process of improving IT service levels provided to the business. While reviews of the individual elements outlined above should be taking place on a quarterly basis, it is likely that, at any particular moment, a review is underway of one or the other IT capability.

Visible measurements

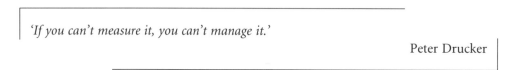

'If you can't measure it, you can't manage it.'

Peter Drucker

As this quote from the late management guru highlights, measurement techniques are a valuable management tool in any domain. There are a number of metrics that can be derived from the principles outlined above, including the following:

- The content and scale of the IT environment, in terms of the services delivered to the business and the technology capabilities that enable them

- Agreed service levels and how well they are being met

- The processes performed by the IT organisation and how well they are performed

- The costs of IT service delivery.

Besides being a valuable tool for IT managers to gain visibility into their own domains, by making metrics public, they also inform the conversation between IT and the business. Says John Johnson, CIO at Intel:

'One of the biggest enablers to effective IT delivery and alignment with the business is building trust and credibility. An important part of this is transparency of costs and visibility of the value delivered, so measurement and metrics are important part of optimising the operational part of the equation.'

There are a number of ways that metrics can be made visible. Besides monthly management reports, consideration should be given to reporting service status on the corporate intranet and, in order to broker a conversation, to encouraging suggestions for additional metrics to be published.

Most importantly of all, don't be tempted to fudge the figures. Measurement is a tool, which is easily blunted if it is treated solely as an exercise in public relations. Equally, reporting of results becomes a motivator: in IT as in sales, people will work harder when a reporting date is being approached, but people will be less likely to perform if it is known or assumed that the figures are massaged in any way.

Remunerate success

People work a lot better if they are pursuing shared goals: this is as true in the IT department as anywhere else. Just as metrics help change behaviour, so does hard cash. IT people have often considered it unfair, perhaps with some justification, that they are often not rewarded on the basis of their performance – if IT is as important to the organisation as people say, then the staff responsible should be able to reap what they sow.

You should consider a bonus scheme that runs across the IT organisation to maximise the likelihood of ongoing effectiveness. Rewards should be established on the basis of providing a trusted service to the business, including, for example:

- Achievement of threshold service levels for core services in line with, and preferably in excess of, business expectations

- Successful resolution of failures which close the gap with business expectations

- Specific activities which improve service levels, for example decommissioning of legacy equipment

- Delivery of projects on time and within budget.

Bonuses do not just change behaviour as activities are completed, but also, people become a great deal more diligent in the specification of activities. It is far more likely that the IT organisation will establish realistic expectations with the business in terms of project and service delivery, if they are to be rewarded for their subsequent achievement.

Summary

- In many organisations, IT is failing to deliver a basic level of capability to the business. This is for a number of reasons, but the result is that IT capabilities often disappoint, while the IT organisation proves itself unable to resolve problems, meet requests or deliver projects effectively. As a result, the business often distrusts the IT organisation and thus finds it difficult to see exactly what value it is adding.

- A significant cause of these difficulties is the fact that IT has traditionally been considered from the point of view of individual technologies and their functions, rather than in terms of the services that are actually experienced. Considering technologies in combination, as services supporting business activities, provides a better starting point for understanding what business expectations of those services are and what is required to meet them.

- With this in mind, a first step in establishing a basic service delivery capability is to conduct a review of how the business is using IT. The review should identify the most critical IT services, how they are delivered and how well – or badly – expectations are being met. Besides being an important information gathering exercise, this step also opens a dialogue between the IT organisation and the business.

- You can use the information from the review as input to understand the costs of IT service delivery and to put in place appropriate procedures to ensure that service levels are maintained. The combination of what the service provides, how well it provides it and how much it costs comprises an agreed service contract between the IT organisation and the business.

- If the lack of trust in IT is due to an absence of service delivery, it is crucial to make a visible, positive impact on the IT services consumed by the business. Quick wins should be followed by improvement projects aimed at fixing higher priority issues, and you should implement ongoing processes of review, audit, reporting and bonus payments to ensure that standards don't slip.

4

Create a common language

The language gap that currently exists between IT organisations and business people is hardly a new phenomenon; industry commentators have talked about it since businesses started using computers. All the same the truth is that for many years the establishment of a common language between IT and business has not been a top priority – not least because there was no need for it to be. Now, however, the pace of IT and business changes and the degree to which IT and business are inextricably woven together in most organisations mean that a shared understanding of goals, strategies, activities, metrics and change implications is a crucial foundation for the delivery of effective IT capabilities. A common language is essential for the establishment and maintenance of that shared understanding.

To some extent, the creation of a shared language between IT and business is simply a matter of hard graft in the direction of cultural and organisational changes. However, there are a handful of important tools that will help you in this endeavour, and we cover them here.

Common areas of misalignment

Language is power

> '*The newest computer can merely compound, at speed, the oldest problem in the relations between human beings, and in the end the communicator will be confronted with the old problem, of what to say and how to say it.*'
>
> Ed Murrow, renowned US journalist and broadcaster, 1908–1965

Language is power, and in the context of IT–business alignment, if the IT organisation is unable to speak the language of business, then ultimately it doesn't have any.

The language of business revolves around money, and here Bob Doyle, former CIO of Kraft Foodservice, explains the challenge:

> '*Everyone in business wants more for less – better, cheaper, faster – and contrary to what you might think, this isn't at all unique to IT. But in a great many organisations IT is often the biggest expense in terms of capital expenditure – and sometimes the largest operational expense, too. This means that IT is often the most visible area for financial management. The challenge is to help board-level executives understand where money is going and how it's being used – and, should they be required, what the effects of cuts might be.*'

The lack of a common language, between IT and businesspeople, means that the IT organisation can only, at best, be a fulfiller of demands – which, in many cases, ends up with IT being seen as a ball-and-chain that is dragged along behind an annoyed and sluggish business entity. As we explain in detail in Chapter 5, this kind of situation is a very poor foundation to try and build sustainable IT–business alignment.

IT value measurement and the return on investment conundrum

> *A warning: if you're of a sensitive disposition, look away now. You might see the following discussion as a form of heresy.*

From the point of view of most businesspeople, it is the business that pays the IT organisation's bills – so surely they should know what they are getting in return?

It is a refrain which recurs almost tediously in our interactions with organisations: business executives bemoan a lack of a comprehensible return on their investments; IT executives, in return, protest that their work is invaluable – but at the same time, struggle to quantify their contribution.

In recent years the IT industry has cottoned onto the fact that IT executives often struggle to explain 'where money is going and how it's being used' (as Bob Doyle points out), and in order to try and help, a kind of micro-industry has been born, helping IT organisations sell their plans to businesspeople in terms of return on investment (ROI) calculations. Case studies for enterprise IT platforms, tools and packaged applications now often centre around ROI estimates, and a number of enterprise IT vendors now offer 'ROI calculators' for their products on their websites.

There's a real problem with this, though, and it's that the formal ROI calculations are rarely the answer (at least, by themselves) for an IT organisation struggling to justify its worth. The truth is that the pursuit of ROI calculations as the primary means of justifying investments is a tempting trap. In actuality it perpetuates the very situation – misaligned IT and business – that so many organisations are trying to get out of.

In situations where there is real trust and understanding between IT and business, formal financial justifications form just one ingredient of much broader investment cases. In such an environment, where the IT organisation has proved itself to be trustworthy, the business sponsors of investments in IT appear to be comfortable about taking recommendations from IT executives at face value. In some situations, formal financial justifications may not be necessary at all.

John Johnson, Intel's CIO, is in an enviable situation of being a highly trusted lieutenant of the CEO, and as a result he's in a position to trust his instincts – and where his instincts are trusted:

'It's important to start off by saying that accountability and transparency in terms of cost and value delivery are absolutely paramount if you are to win the trust of the business, so the mechanics for measuring this need to be an inherent part of the way you run the IT function.

Having said this, we run the risk of ROI constipation sometimes. In some situations, you just have to follow your instincts, and we've just completed a major collaboration technology rollout that was one of those. Even today, I am not sure I could tell you how to calculate the value of this technology across the organisation, but there is no doubt that value is being added. I sometimes envy small businesses which are able to work on a gut feel basis without the need to go through formal analysis of ROI, NPV, TCO, etc. Sometimes it is very obvious what needs to be done, even though you would have no idea how to construct an Excel spreadsheet to prove it.'

There is a 'trust gap' between business and IT in a great many organisations, and the sustainable way to bridge the gap, having first established a base level of trust as we discuss in Chapter 3, isn't to focus heavily on trying to engineer financial justifications for all IT investments – it's to build a common shared language between IT and business. Yes, there are aspects of this language which need to have a financial flavour, But that's because money is integral to the language of business; financial justification isn't an end in itself.

Financial calculations alone are becoming less able to measure IT value

ROI, Net Present Value (NPV) and other investment value estimation tools are useful in calculating returns from 'traditional' capital investments – things like investing in new machinery (for a manufacturer) or new aeroplanes (for an airline). They help to answer the question: is this investment going to make me more money than if I just left my cash in the bank?

It's comparatively easy, for example, for a supermarket chain to estimate the ROI of opening a new supermarket. It's probably opened 500 supermarkets before and has collected a lot of information along the way about how much does running a supermarket cost, including information about how a new opening affects demand at other stores that are within striking distance.

The problem with IT investments however is that increasingly, they just do not lend themselves well to simplistic analysis. There are three challenges in particular:

- *Scope*: as we discuss in detail in Chapter 6, increasingly, as businesses become more heavily saturated with IT systems, the boundaries between investments are blurring as systems 'bump into each other'. As a result investments have effects beyond the scope that they are typically considered within. The resulting 'fuzzy edges' of investment returns make the definition of the scope of an investment value calculation difficult to do.

- *Stakeholders*: it's a truism that 'where you sit governs what you see'. As the boundaries of IT investments blur into each other, so the number and variety of stakeholders who have an interest in each investment increase. Every stakeholder has their own goals with their own scope and their own set of ideas about how they will measure progress towards those goals. Do you have to do ROI for each stakeholder?

- *Avoided costs and intangible value*: a great many ROI estimates are based on estimates of 'cost avoided' – in other words, the assumption is that return on an investment comes from savings achieved, relative to the expenditure that would've been made if you'd 'done nothing'. Putting aside the major challenge associated with this model that comes from the fact that you can only get a decent input to this kind of estimate if you have already gathered sound statistics on the alternative 'do nothing' working mode, the broader challenge with this model is that the link between today's common

IT investments and easy-to-identify savings is a tenuous one. Often, the value of IT investments can be subtle, with manifold elements – and the intended result is only partly about savings; partly or mostly the intended result is about fulfilling the organisation's strategy and driving innovations and new opportunities.

On the last point, eminent authors Bob Kaplan and David Norton explain in their book 'Strategy Maps – Converting Intangible Assets into Tangible Outcomes' that the primary assets that result from IT investments are intangible – comprising various forms of human, organisational and information capital. In particular, they explain how:

> *'None of these intangible assets has value that can be measured separately or independently. The value of these intangible assets derives from their ability to help the organization implement its strategy... Intangible assets such as knowledge and technology seldom have a direct impact on financial outcomes such as increased revenues, lowered costs, and higher profits. Improvements in intangible assets affect financial outcomes through chains of cause-and-effect relationships.'*

To take this further, even if you can do an ROI estimate that makes sense, all you're doing is estimating the tangible elements of the investment return. Increasingly, as the focus of automation moves away from structured, stable back office processes (where, principally, ROI can absolutely be estimated based on costs avoided as a result of automation) towards dynamic, informal front office practices, the value of IT investment tips very firmly away from easily estimated costs avoided, in favour of intangible value elements such as improved collaboration, improved customer satisfaction and so on.

The supermarket example above highlights another weakness with the use of ROI analysis for IT investments. Organisations rarely revisit the analysis after implementation to measure the returns which were actually achieved. This is in part due not only to the very challenges outlined above but also because ROI is seen as a necessary evil to obtain investment funding rather than a means of informing future investment decisions.

In summary, a heavy focus on formal financial justification is a behaviour that feels like an easy way out of what is really a deeper challenge. The real challenge is broader, and it is that the value of IT is invisible to businesspeople because IT activity is poorly understood. The real answer is to create new conversations to develop that understanding, rather than trying to justify yourself in the context of the old ones.

Many specialisms, many languages

It's abundantly clear that business and IT people speak different languages. It is more complicated than that, however: in truth, a broader range of business and technical communities speak a wide variety of languages.

Business departments and IT teams alike are specialised units. They've got this way because in many cases, specialisation is vital to success. Business teams have specialised skills in finance, purchasing or marketing for example, whereas technology teams have specialised skills in database administration or Java software development.

And these multiple technology and business domains each have their own specialised jargon. Financial boffins talk about NPV, EBITDA and CAGR; marketing 'heads' talk about above- and below-the-line marketing, the 'marketing mix', MLM and logical adjacencies; and purchasing wonks talk about BVRs, PQQs, RFIs and the effects of TUPE. Technology geeks, of course, are never happier than when talking about JEE, OOP, refactoring, ESBs and so on. The IT industry is one with jargon at its very heart.

Of course, in order to communicate within business circles, business specialists already speak a common, general purpose business language. Likewise, the vast majority of IT specialists speak a common, general purpose IT language in addition to their own specialist dialects.

Figure 4.1 illustrates this profusion of languages and illustrates the obvious corollary of this profusion of specialised languages: creating a common language between IT and business has to be an endeavour that seeks to find common ground, rather than one that attempts to educate businesspeople about the details of various aspects of IT. The profusion of specialised languages that exists in businesses can't be whittled away; the solution is to build bridges, not to attempt to flatten the landscape.

The figure shows the two types of language bridges that can reasonably, and which need to be, built between IT and business.

First, it's necessary to build a bridge between general purpose IT and business languages – particularly, to allow those people at the heads of IT and business teams to talk in a way

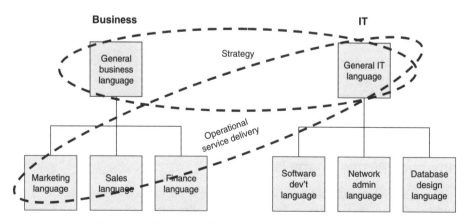

Figure 4.1: The scope of a common IT–business language

which makes sense to them all. This bridge is essential to effective strategy and roadmap planning, as we explain in Chapter 6.

With that bridge built, it's very important to build others between a general purpose IT language and the languages used by individual business specialisms to ensure effective communication between IT and business in operational situations, where the main concern is ensuring that ongoing service delivery meets the needs of the people who take advantage of those services. We deal with the organisational aspects of this in detail in Chapter 5, but in short a critical success factor for IT–business alignment is to provide a 'layer' of IT staff which is responsible for representing IT services to business teams, acting as service managers throughout the life cycles of IT investments. These IT staff members *have* to be able to converse with business people in terms which enable them to really capture requirements and feedback effectively.

One symptom of this language incompatibility is that IT responsibilities are very often not defined in terms that make sense to business people.

Bob Doyle, former CIO of Kraft Foodservice, illustrates this:

'Often there is a poor organisational structure in IT that bears no relationship to the customer's needs. There's a real misunderstanding of the business and even the business of IT. There's still a focus on speeds and feeds. People need to be educated that "your job is to make sure claims are processed quickly," and so on – not that "your job is to keep the servers up." '

When is communication not communication?

In our research for this book as well as in our history of working with organisations of all types, we've noted another common symptom of the lack of a trusted relationship between IT and business: the IT organisation is overly reliant on electronic rather than personal communication: e-mail is favoured over face-to-face meetings or conference calls.

E-mail creates a cushion between a sender and a receiver; it's possible to run away from bad news, at least for a while, just as someone might run away after lobbing a grenade into an enemy bunker. But e-mail is very rarely a very quick way to get things done, particularly if the objective needs some kind of formal commitment from a number of parties. The indirection that makes e-mail attractive when breaking bad news also makes it easy for people being asked to do things to avoid doing them. E-mail is also very poor at conveying other elements that are critical to human communication, including nuance, emphasis, irony and, of course, body language and so introduces a far greater risk of misunderstanding and misinterpretation.

Adam Overfield, Managing Director of renewable energy provider Pure Power, supports this view strongly:

> *'I think we've become a bit obsessed with sharing information, to the point where it's become stupid. The amount of information that was thrown at us at my previous company was just amazing. Email after email, people just stopped reading them. What caused real frustration was, a few weeks later there may be a staff meeting, somebody may ask a question from the floor and the guy who was chairing the staff meeting would say, 'well, there was a communication about that 3 weeks ago. You should be reading your emails, it's our primary form of communication, you're obviously not doing it, I suggest you do!' I saw that happen 3 or 4 times, of course it just turns your staff off completely. So – it can be used as a tool that senior managers can hide behind and almost remove themselves from having to deal with the nitty gritty, day to day.'*

Business needs to learn IT too, doesn't it?

Although a lot of the blame for miscommunication and lack of trust between business and IT teams can be laid at the IT organisation's door, it would be a huge oversimplification to ignore the responsibility that business leaders have to learn a little about IT – particularly in terms of language.

Twenty years ago it would have been absolutely valid for business executives to counter this kind of assertion robustly: 'Why on earth should I care about IT? I'm in charge of merchandising, not IT. And we're a retailer, not a software company'. Today, though, this argument just doesn't wash. No matter what industry you're in and no matter the size of the company you work for, knowing a little about IT is a fundamental prerequisite for being able to do your job effectively. IT is a fundamental pillar of business infrastructure, like finance. IT supports every business area, directly and indirectly. All business executives know something about financial matters; why don't they know a similar amount about IT?

Darin Brumby, CIO of First Group, explains that IT knowledge within a business leadership team is critically important:

> *'Boards have been complicit in what they have not done, with this element [IT] of their organisations. The fact that they don't know about it, they didn't grow up with it, they didn't learn about it in University – that won't wash. They are leading major corporations, and to do that they need to have oversight of every element of the organisation.*
>
> *Of course, we want to have experts in key areas, but if you don't understand IT, learn, read up, educate yourself, get better, have the dialogue, the resulting situation will be*

unsustainable. Education about IT hasn't happened enough in business from those other parts of the organisation which have overall responsibility and accountability for integrating talent, to achieve, I don't want to be pedantic but at the end of the day to make money, that hasn't happened enough. And it hasn't happened enough, because sometimes these business leaders haven't trusted where they are getting the information from.'

Brumby is saying that trust is a key element to bootstrapping the IT–business relationship (something that came up time and again in our research). In other words, we can't expect business leaders to take responsibility for learning a little about IT, until the IT organisation makes an effort to show that it's worth trusting. We talked about key aspects of creating trust in Chapter 3, but a major precursor to trust is communication, and effective communication means that IT and business have to come together.

Graeme Hackland, IT Manager for the Renault F1 team, might just be the exception that proves the rule. The Renault F1 team is a very technical organisation, led by engineers, and so communication between IT and business is comparatively straightforward. Still, it's critical that he explains how IT investments are actually benefiting the business:

'I don't feel the need to sit in board meetings, to discuss how we're going to win races, do our marketing, and so on. What's far more effective is to be in the level below – to be part of the technology management team, but not part of the board.

I think we're lucky that the management group all understand the value IT brings to the business, because they're all technology people. It's down to us to make them all aware of what we're doing and how it benefits, though.'

Alignment imperatives

As we have already said, many of the challenging situations that IT organisations – and by implication, businesses more broadly – face, come down to a lack of trust between business and IT. A lot of that lack of trust is down to a lack of visibility – onto what is spent on IT, where it goes and what is the business result. And that lack of visibility, in the end, can't be addressed by engineering financial justifications of IT investments in isolation. It can only be addressed by changing the kinds of conversation that occur between business and IT executives.

The first step in establishing that trust is for someone to initiate the conversation – and that someone has to be the IT organisation. The results of any conversation are important, but the quality of those results and the commitment of the participants to them depends on how effective the conversation is. It is important therefore to avoid the tendency to focus on the output, be it an ROI justification, a business strategy or a set of technical standards, at the expense of the process which creates it. The process will help to break down any language barriers that will constrain the quality of the output. Shared commitment also demands involvement from those with something to contribute. Equally, those individuals must feel they are getting something back for what they are putting in.

Ultimately, what's needed is an ongoing dialogue based on a shared grammar, which is encouraged by example and through reward.

Achieving alignment

Between business and IT, IT has to make the first move

Businesspeople might have some responsibility to make an effort and learn a degree of IT language, but the onus is definitely on IT organisations to make the first move, since it has got to show it's worth trusting – see Figure 4.2 below.

This is a challenge because in a great many IT organisations it is technical expertise rather than 'soft' people skills, which have been the mark of progression within IT ranks. Historically IT organisations, business and people skills just haven't been valued in the same way that software design skills, for example, have. A common result is that staff managers, service line managers and business relationship managers within IT organisations are seen by technologists as second-class citizens – not smart enough to be 'real IT people' – and are given little serious consideration.

Figure 4.2: IT has to make the first move

Nick Malik, Enterprise Architect, Microsoft, is clear on this point from his own experience at the software behemoth (where there are over 6000 people employed in IT alone):

> *'Really engaging with the business is a problem for a lot of companies because frankly in the IT industry we've spent far too much time promoting geeks and nerds. Getting ahead in IT has for too long been about knowing all about messaging middleware and not enough about being able to really explain things to businesspeople and listen to their needs – and frame solutions to problems in terms of business strategy.*
>
> *If you want to be in a leadership position in IT inside microsoft, you have to be able to communicate with business. Business people in Microsoft have no time for IT people who can't relate to them on a peer level, and push back when they're being asked to do something stupid.'*

Enterprise architecture: the dictionary for the business–IT interface

We could give the topic of enterprise architecture (EA) a book in its own right (indeed, a large number of books have been written on the topic already). It's not our goal in this chapter to give a detailed exposition of the principles or practice of EA, rather what we want to do is illustrate the central role that an EA practice has to play in any IT–business alignment effort, in creating the foundation of a common language.

The commonly held view of EA is that its value comes from constraints that it places on the procurement, development and integration of IT capabilities. This view focuses on the role of EA teams as 'policemen' of sorts – acting as key influencers on the operation of IT management processes, by setting policies that seek to reconcile the kinds of short-term pressures that impinge on business-driven IT projects with a long-term view of how the IT portfolio overall has to develop to support business strategy.

Sally Bean, a senior enterprise architect working for a number of global industry clients, explains this view:

> *'EA is about blueprinting and rationalisation – it's about creating descriptions of IT and the business which allow you to make intelligent decisions. This involves creating as-is and to-be pictures. The outcome should be a kind of 'storyboard' for having*

> conversations – providing input to infrastructure rationalisation, project portfolio management, and so on.'

This perspective on the value of EA is absolutely valid and correct, and indeed it should be a key input into the IT Governance Board (ITGB) process we talk about in Chapter 6. But it only presents one part of the value of EA work. The perspective is partial because it focuses exclusively on the work's outputs. From our research we're confident that the value of EA doesn't only come from the outputs of EA work and how they're used to constrain other processes, but also from the EA process itself.

That's because the EA process, done right, questions, discovers, refines and documents the key principles that guide the organisation as a whole – and works to understand how the IT organisation currently supports those principles and how that level of support can be improved. The process of questioning, discovery, refinement and documentation itself can bring stakeholders with diverse backgrounds together, having conversations about how things really work and how IT should be supporting them. This helps to build the bridges at the strategic and operational levels we discussed earlier.

A critical success factor here, though, is that the EA process is conducted in a way that encourages widespread participation, communication and feedback.

Enterprise architecture: scope and scale

It's worth getting a bit crisper about what we mean by EA. This is important because there appears to be a bit of confusion in industry about what EA is. Specifically, there are two camps. The difference between them is in how they interpret the word 'enterprise':

- One sees the 'enterprise' in EA as being about scale – EA is about architecting systems that span the enterprise.

- The other sees the 'enterprise' in EA as being about scope – EA is about not just the consideration of IT capabilities and their development but also of business models and strategies too.

We absolutely subscribe to the latter view.

EA process: ivory towers versus consensus building

When setting out to create an EA capability in your organisation, it's tempting to employ the brightest thinkers who have demonstrated a great ability to hold huge amounts of information in their heads at once, and make sense of it all. After all, IT environments these days are complex and only becoming more so. Describing and analysing these environments takes real skill. Then, you set those thinkers free to embark on a kind of 'EA discovery' journey, where they set the terms of reference for the new EA practice and tailor one of the existing EA frameworks and models used in industry to suit their own needs.

The challenge with this approach is that it's very easy for a team like this to isolate itself – to set itself above and apart from IT development and operational teams, and also from business executives. The team produces a stream of documentation. Nobody reads it or takes any notice of it whatsoever. The team is into its stride now, modelling every nuance of the IT environment and how it relates to business operations (although in reality it doesn't do very much of this stuff, it instead concentrates on accurately modelling the current and future state of the IT environment).

This kind of 'ivory tower' EA activity occurs in practice far too often. The EA team is first distrusted and then ignored. EA becomes an expensive failure, and the organisation becomes disenchanted with the value of EA and chalks up the whole experience as a failed experiment.

The kind of people who are naturally skilled at, and interested in, modelling are smart people. But they're not necessarily the kind of people who feel comfortable collaborating with others. And this is the big problem because for the EA process to deliver real business value at its core, it has to be about not only gathering information in order to produce models but also sharing information and insight to shape those models.

A dictionary is of no value unless it's read and used, and in large organisations people will only put the time into 'reading the dictionary' if they feel they have some skin in the game. This means that in order to be successful, an EA process has to 'export' information at the same time as 'importing' it. As illustrated in Figure 4.3, rather than just sucking information out of business and IT stakeholders in the kind of interview-type situations that commonly dominate system requirements gathering exercises, EA practitioners have to be able to give and take information, so that both parties learn something. Working this way takes longer, but the value is much greater. As the EA practitioner works with stakeholders in this way, they are helping to foster a shared understanding amongst the stakeholder community of the key business and IT concepts that comprise the dictionary for our common language.

This is not an easy thing to get right. It involves EA practitioners being willing to 'give up control' and to share their ideas and thoughts before they're 100% baked. That's not something that many EA types are naturally predisposed to do.

The other important factor in the success of an EA process in getting buy-in and building a common language that really works is the EA practitioners' ability to look beyond model-ling as an exercise in itself and preparedness to be influenced by key technology trends, patterns and standards being brought into the organisation through procurement of off-the-shelf packaged applications, hosted services or externally developed custom systems.

It's crucial to remember that the goal of EA is not to design the perfect set of custom-built IT capabilities according to the architectural approaches and technology

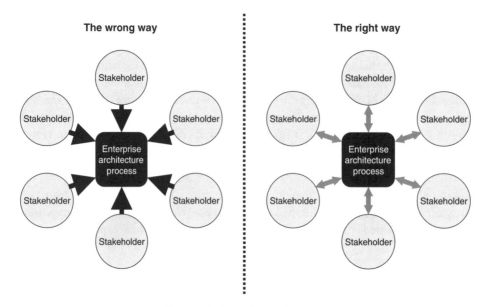

Figure 4.3: EA rights and wrongs

platforms that the architects believe are the absolute best, but it's about optimising a multifaceted equation that has to take account of the sourcing strategy of the organisation, the technology directions of key suppliers and directions of the technology industry in general (particularly in terms of technology standards). Service Oriented Architecture (SOA) is a case in point: if your organisation is a customer of one of the major packaged business application vendors, your IT environment will be injected with a significant dose of SOA sooner or later, whether the EA team likes it or not. Every EA team should be thinking about the impact of SOA on its organisation's IT landscape because SAP, Oracle, Microsoft and all the other significant players are currently going down the path of deconstructing their application suites into sets of services which can be easily configured and composed to allow for easier integration and better functional flexibility.

From a practical perspective, while modelling and documentation is important and valuable in many situations, the lesson is to keep your eye on the ball and not get too obsessed with trying to analyse, model and redesign everything from first principles for the sake of it. In many areas it just isn't worth it, and in others, the model will never keep up with the business.

Don't boil the ocean

As discussed above, one of the risks of setting the EA team free is that they attempt to model everything. As the EA process begins to build the bridges at the strategic and operational level, it will help to identify and prioritise particular business and IT initiatives and thus focus efforts.

The EA team should be responsible for enterprise-wide business–IT modelling; they just should not attempt to do it all at once. Instead, by focussing on particular initiatives and working incrementally, it is more likely that results will be achieved in the required time frame. This more agile, iterative approach will also make it easier to measure and demonstrate success.

Language and the IT investment life cycle

The IT organisation isn't in the business of developing applications for business people to use; it's in the business of delivering services that support business activity. This highlights a crucial but subtle issue – and one which much of the discussion about SOA overlooks.

A service is something you experience, not just something you build. A service-oriented approach to IT capability delivery necessitates a whole life cycle approach to IT investment. It should enable a 'continuity of intent' in discussions between business and IT organisations, all the way from investment through delivery, to change management. In this context, it's the start of a consistent model for planning and designing, and then measuring IT work effectiveness that will make sense to business.

But there's more to it than just saying 'the answer is to follow a service-oriented approach'. Really, creating a common IT and business language that works through the IT investment-delivery-change cycle means you have to focus relentlessly on getting everyone pitching conversations at the right level.

Money talks!

Having railed against the value of relying on formal ROI estimates to justify investments, it's nevertheless clear from our research for this book that being able to talk about financial costs and business benefits is a crucially important part of the overall language that IT organisations have to develop. Whether you're having conversations about IT investment, giving feedback to stakeholders about how well the system resulting from an investment is delivering value or working through the complexities of how to change that system, you have to be able to talk to business people in terms that make sense to them – and the language of business revolves around money. Every business executive worth his/ her salt knows how much he/she is spending on particular programmes (offering promotions to reduce customer churn, for example) and is able to measure the outcomes of those programmes (reduced customer churn, hopefully).

Angela Yochem, the vice president of Portfolio Architecture for SunTrust Banks, is convinced that in order to be relevant, you have to be comfortable about talking about money:

> *'With everything you do, the impact should be measurable, or at least estimable. And if you're trying to talk to the business you have to know the soft costs as well as the hard costs of what you do – and to be able to apply this knowledge to potential decisions.'*

Carson Booth, IT Director EMEA at Starwood Hotels, gets to the root of the issue:

> *'It's a mutual education – we're trying to educate but we're currently speaking a language customers don't understand. We need to try to use the normal business lingo rather than technical lingo to explain things. Business managers don't want to talk about DOS and Windows, they want to talk about things they understand. Most people understand financial terminology, so that's a good start.'*

. . .But formal financial justification isn't always what's needed

We explained earlier that a heavy focus on formal financial justification is quite often a symptom of a lack of trust between IT and business. The truth is that often it's just not relevant to try and formally quantify a financial return for an investment – the benefit of doing this itself has no business justification.

A great example of this kind of situation is where an IT investment is required to help the organisation match a new offer from a competitor. As long as the cost isn't completely prohibitive, it's likely that the most important thing will be to get the organisation on par with its competitor, sooner rather than later. In order to be able to understand these parameters, of course, you have to be able to talk to business executives to find out exactly *how* important it is that the organisation matches its competitor's offer and, of course, you also have to be able to understand what kind of cost the business executives will see as *completely prohibitive* (it's all subjective, to a degree – and only they can tell you).

Our research on senior IT executives who have built trusted relationships with their business peers shows that where trust exists, it's possible to work based on less of a formal financial footing. Business executives trust that the IT executives' explanations of business value of investments are sound.

Bob Doyle, former CIO of Kraft Foodservice, explains:

> *'There are investments that demand clear return – such as spending $100m on revamping a manufacturing process – but there are lots of other things where the benefits are more varied and much 'softer'. Moreover sometimes the driver for an investment is actually about keeping up with the competition or with regulation.*

Where I've traditionally got in trouble around ROI was when the business owner hasn't been tied into the process of the project/programme. Unless you get the relevant business exec(s) involved at the start and at the end of a project you can't really get a handle on issues concerning benefits/returns, outcomes. Moreover if you do have real involvement from the business then buy-in is much easier regardless of the presentation of a formal ROI analysis.'

John Johnson, Intel's CIO, agrees that a trusted peer relationship can make the business of selling IT investments much easier:

'If you have a model in place which allows you to deliver value to the business in a positive, measurable and consistent way, you earn the right to go with your instincts on specific initiatives from time to time.

Something that makes these kinds of decisions much easier is working in genuine partnership with the business. You can then make these kinds of judgment calls much more easily knowing that you are in tune or at least heading in the right kind of general direction to deliver something the business needs or is likely to need in future.'

Talk about business, not IT, performance measurement

The principal challenge in this area of communicating in business-meaningful terms comes when your IT organisation is looking to provide feedback about the operational performance of IT investments. Given the systems monitoring and management tools that are in place in most IT organisations, it's very tempting to provide feedback about 'service levels' that is technical rather than business-meaningful in nature. Even when IT teams try and step up to the plate of giving useful feedback about the value of investments, they talk the language of technology rather than business.

Bob Doyle, former CIO of Kraft Foodservice, provides an example:

'Feedback has to be in business meaningful, rather than IT terms – so measurements have to be about the business impact of IT performance, not IT performance itself. For example give people feedback about how IT is supporting on-time deliveries, improving scores on customer surveys, shortening claims processing times, and so on. You can back these up with technical service levels if required but they're not the top level issue you should be focusing on.'

Malcolm Whitehouse, IS director and CIO in the UK Government's Department of Work and Pensions (DWP), agrees:

> *'In order to demonstrate that IT is currently delivering business value, there is no point discussing IT capabilities and quality-of-service in terms of servers, networks and so forth. You need to discuss it in terms of end-to-end business capabilities, in order to demonstrate understanding of what the business does. You have to be able to relate the metrics used to measure and demonstrate IT performance to those metrics used by the business to measure the business performance.'*

There is a crucial technology element here – you need a monitoring and management system in place that observes important operational events in the IT infrastructure and analyses those events using knowledge of the relationships between technologies, services and business processes in order to highlight the higher level business impact. IT Service Management (ITSM) tools can help here.

But it's a case of garbage in, garbage out. ITSM tools can only make accurate inferences if they're configured with information about how individual pieces of infrastructure inter-relate and support applications, business processes and business operations. EA work is critical in uncovering these relationships because the EA process, if done right, will uncover these all important linkages.

Language in the wild: avoiding 'technobabble'

Good technology people are passionate about technology – and many of them are very detail-orientated. They don't always understand that not everyone else shares their love of the nuts and bolts. Some of them also use technology terminology as a way of demonstrating their expertise and experience and look down on people who don't 'get it'.

But we all know that at the end of the day, *it doesn't matter*. No, a sales manager couldn't redesign a Java application to use dependency injection and aspect-oriented patterns to save their lives, but it's also extraordinarily unlikely that a Java programmer would be able to motivate a team of salespeople to beat their quarterly target. And it's the salespeople who bring in the money that pays the Java programmer's salary.

Avoiding 'technobabble' in conversations with businesspeople – or even with IT people not familiar with your particular area of expertise – is the most elementary thing that anyone in the IT organisation can do to improve IT–business alignment. One of the key action points here is to think carefully about the terms that get used and coach technologists to replace them with other terms or short descriptions.

The important thing, though, so as not to alienate technologists, is to make sure that any work you do here is as much aimed at businesspeople (helping them understand geek-speak) as it is at technologists (encouraging them to use descriptions that make sense to laymen).

Work towards 'what', not 'how'

Often in IT the acronyms and technology descriptions that stick, describe how things are built rather than describing the resulting capability. In short it's about how, not what. To succeed we need to turn this around and get people talking about 'what', not 'how'.

A great current example of this focus on 'how', rather than 'what', is 'composite applications'. Think about it. That says a lot about how systems are put together and virtually nothing about what the result actually means for a user.

The good news is that businesspeople understand some concepts which have become part of the technology landscape innately – particularly the concepts of 'business process' and 'managed service', which can and should form the conceptual framework at the heart of your EA work (we discuss this in detail in Chapter 9). Figure 4.4 provides some more examples.

Technobabble!	Try...
Web services	Integration of systems using standards, which will work within our company or even between us and our partners and suppliers
SOA	A way of delivering IT capabilities that makes it much easier to make changes quickly, and share common capabilities across different systems, reducing cost and risk
Composite applications	Role-based interfaces to systems and information sources that bring all the stuff you need to carry out your job together in one place
Federated identity	A way of allowing users in our company to login once and gain access to the systems they need at our trusted partners – and vice versa
Server virtualisation	Technology that makes it possible to utilise our server hardware much more efficiently

Figure 4.4: Technobabble and its translation

Maintaining alignment

Building sustainability into the common language

The major challenge in building a common language that can be shared across business and IT constituencies is how to make any improvements or initiatives you undertake sustainable. Changing the type of conversations that business and IT people engage in is a question of changing ingrained habits, and we all know that old habits die hard. Below we outline five hurdles that often present themselves, together with some tips to help you overcome them.

Get EA programme funding

As is also the case in the material we cover in Chapter 6, getting line-of-business executives to commit funding to shared IT capabilities and resources can be an uphill struggle. This is understandable: it's common for divisions and departments to focus laser-like on their own performance – not least because that's how they are measured and rewarded – so anything which doesn't have an immediately understandable impact on that performance moves down the priority list.

Of course, EA activity can be funded solely within an existing IT budget. But unless you have a particularly large IT department, funding an EA programme 'under the radar', even if you can manage it by trimming expenditure elsewhere, is going to have a negative impacts the resources available for other projects. For this reason (and also for the reason that you might be able to secure ring-fenced funding) it makes sense to make a funding case for EA as an explicit activity with strategic value to the organisation.

In order to do this it's crucial to focus on how EA adds value to the organisation, by explaining that EA is not just about modelling and navel-gazing, but it's a tool that enables the IT organisation to effectively understand and support the organisation's strategic objectives. If you take time to look at the organisation's overall strategy, it's highly likely that you'll uncover one or more objectives that demand co-ordination and integration between the operations of different parts of the business. EA's role is central to the achievement of these strategic objectives.

Of course, the linkage of EA's value to cross-cutting, strategic, organisational objectives means that it's going to be tough to convince divisional and departmental heads without some extra help. No, to really make a case for EA you'll have to go up to the board level – above the divisional business unit heads – and sell the idea. Having a CIO at board level, as we discuss in Chapter 5, helps here. Regardless of whether the CIO is 'at the top', a critical success factor of EA initiatives is that all the senior executives who sign up to the need for EA need to actively participate in driving the mandate down through the management layers.

Make EA actionable, not passive

We explained earlier in this chapter that it's imperative to pursue the process of 'doing' EA in an open, rather than closed, way – looking to build consensus rather than an ivory tower and also taking account of technology and other trends which are likely to be imposed on the organisation via the acquisition of tools, platforms, applications and services from external providers.

On top of these EA success factors, there's another factor which is very important to consider if your EA initiative is to have a viable lifespan: making EA actionable.

It's very tempting for EA practitioners to focus on the big picture stuff, modelling as-is and to-be IT landscapes and mapping out how these support key business operations. However modelling states isn't enough, although if the process is conducted openly it will help socialise some common language concepts: EA also has to get actively involved in setting out how the organisation will get from 'as-is' to 'to-be'. EA has to be actionable, in other words. This should happen through collaboration with the ITGB process (we discuss this in more detail, in Chapter 6 principle).

An EA practice that doesn't look beyond modelling is no different in reality from the teams which created the, largely unsuccessful, corporate data models of 20 years ago.

Define EA performance criteria

Another potential 'gotcha' when creating an EA capability comes from the fact that EA is not a process with a defined end-point. You can't consider EA as a project or even a programme; in order to have long-term value you have to consider it as a perpetual process – a practice, like that in your law or marketing department.

To ensure that a process of this kind delivers long-term value, a 'continuous improvement' approach is the order of the day. If your EA capability is initiated but never monitored, its value won't be measured. And without regular feedback about the value that EA is adding, sponsors (and those who need to be influenced by EA work) will slowly become less and less interested in what EA practitioners have to say.

The first thing is to define some performance criteria that can be used to measure EA's effectiveness. These will likely vary from organisation to organisation, but whatever the quirks of your own organisation might be, performance criteria are likely to be most useful when they measure EA's contribution to strategic objectives that cut across the IT footprints that support multiple business processes, departments and divisions.

You might choose to develop criteria that measure performance in the following areas:

- To what degree is the EA capability seen as a source of organisation-wide expertise in how business and IT connect?

- How many business and IT stakeholders are engaged in conversations with EA practitioners?

- Do business and IT stakeholders feel that EA practitioners help them understand the interconnections between business and IT operations and capabilities?

- Are the EA process' outputs widely understood?

- Is the EA team effective in reshaping project terms of reference, requirements and other criteria?

- Is the EA team instrumental in killing "bad" projects and/or encouraging them to be reworked?

- Is the EA process leading to tangible results such as increased utilisation of shared services and rationalisation and consolidation of IT infrastructure?

- Are business stakeholders able to understand and make decisions based on the performance metrics provided by the IT organisation?

Note that these criteria aren't the kind that you can measure directly, objectively and quantitatively (at least, not very easily). That means you need to find other ways of getting input. Benchmarking surveys are a good option.

Once you've defined a set of EA performance criteria that make sense for your organisation, you need to use these to measure the success of EA at regular intervals. An annual review cycle is a good start.

Make face-to-face communication the rule not the exception

We explained earlier the risks inherent in reliance on electronic communications. As John Johnson, CIO of Intel, points out:

'Communication is the key to dealing with pretty much all the softer issues. We have a general rule that if there is a need to discuss priorities or trade-offs, that kind of thing, then the conversation has to take place either over the phone or face-to-face. It is a simple thing but I see so many instances of conflict occurring because people have tried to use email for the wrong kinds of things. I admit that this is a real challenge to implement, as email is often the default way for many people to communicate internally, but my advice to anyone who really wants to manage the softer relationship issues is just to make sure that people talk to each other. Everything else falls into place if you do this.'

The challenge, of course, is exactly how *'to make sure that people talk to each other'*. The first step is to lead by example. If senior business and IT personnel step away from the keyboard and actively engage in discussions and respond to e-mail requests with polite suggestions to meet face-to-face then word will get round. That can only go so far, so it needs to be made clear that important decisions can only be taken as a result of meetings, particularly where those decisions involve softer issues. Finally, ensure that the correct behaviour is acknowledged and rewarded as part of the performance review process.

Get more than lip service from staff

It's easy to get staff to pay lip service to an initiative to get IT and business using more comprehensible language in each others' presence and seeking to use common models of IT and business as terms of reference when discussing investments, requirements and so on.

But it's much harder to get everyone to stick to the initiative over weeks, months and years. What do you do if staff continue in their old ways and refuse to engage in the way that they need to? There's only one thing to do and it doesn't require fancy thinking or techniques to carry out. Reward the right behaviour in performance appraisals – using feedback gained from the business and IT stakeholders that individuals interact within their daily jobs. Make it clear to any individuals who are failing in this regard due to lack of commitment that they need to shape up or ship out.

When all's said and done, there are very few IT roles where antisocial individuals, no matter how smart, can be valued members of the organisation.

Summary

- Trust between IT and business is the key foundation stone of sustainable IT-business alignment, but trust can't be fostered unless both sides understand each other – and for that IT and business practitioners need to share a common language. However specialisation in both IT and business is crucial to organisational effectiveness, and specialists tend to have their own languages. This means that the primary goal here is to build bridges rather than flatten the landscape. Success will come from individuals learning a new language rather than forgetting their existing languages.

- Enterprise Architecture practice plays a central role in building the common language which enables IT and business practitioners to establish and maintain effective relationships. But it's vital that EA is itself governed in a way that fosters business focus and sustainable value. These will come when an EA programme is conducted in an open, didactic fashion and when its value is clearly monitored and measured to drive continuous improvement.

- Beyond the initiation of an effective EA practice, there are a number of smaller, but equally crucial, changes that you can make to the way that the IT organisation interacts with business communities, sponsors and stakeholders. Most important amongst these are the use of business terms and business-meaningful metrics when providing operational feedback on services; getting technologists to replace their technology jargon – the 'how' – with descriptions of technologies and services which will make sense to service consumers – the 'what'; and promoting face-to-face communication over e-mail communication. These changes are all about behaviour, however, you will have to make sure you align reward and appraisal processes with these goals to see sustainable change.

5

Establish a peer relationship between business and IT

It's very difficult indeed to create IT–business alignment that is sustainable in the long term if there isn't a high degree of mutual trust between multiple points in both IT and business teams. This kind of trust is obtained through the creation of a common language and the establishment of shared goals and objectives, and of course an environment where basic IT service delivery 'just works'. But on top of this foundation of trust there needs to be real sharing of authority and responsibility when it comes to making and implementing decisions that have implications for business and IT. This requires a serious commitment to make some key changes in the IT organisation, business departments and the boardroom.

Given this trust, this section explores how IT can move away from a subservient role towards a peer relationship, enabling IT to take responsibility for its own domain and recognising that the business needs in-house technology understanding. This comes about through a deep commitment by IT and business to engage both at a strategic level and an operational level.

Common areas of misalignment

Suppliers do what they're told

> *'In the past, business units defined what they wanted, threw it over the desk, and waited for the result. SBB's ICT group is now reorganising to take a radically different approach, but it has to convince business units that IT understands the business and that it can really help.*
>
> *Most IT guys don't have the right kinds of communication skills; they are quite happy to be seen as "passive" IT suppliers who just accept a request and do their best. But this doesn't fit with what the business leadership really wants from IT – they want IT to help with innovation and drive the business forward.'*
>
> Andreas Dietrich, CIO, SBB

The foundation principle for creating sustainable IT–business alignment is to start building trust in the business that IT is able to 'get the basics right'. An IT organisation has to be able to make simple service commitments and deliver based on them – and if it can't do that, then there's no hope of anything else more sophisticated happening.

However, a focus on 'getting the basics right' leads you towards a model of 'IT as supplier'. And although this idea has merit, it's not enough to ensure sustainable IT–business alignment. The 'IT as supplier' model is necessary, but not sufficient.

Why? Because suppliers, by definition, do what they're told. The customer is always right! The parameters of service delivery are defined by the 'customer', and thereafter the supplier delivers, in response to requests, in the context of those parameters (you can think of these as 'contracts' and 'service-level agreements').

This is an absolutely reasonable and professional way to go about things, but it's only the start. IT is woven into the fabric of most key business processes, and business change is perpetual. It's possible to keep the business happy in day-to-day operations by playing a supplier role, but in order for IT to be really effective at supporting the business strategically, that supplier role has to be augmented with other capabilities, activities and responsibilities.

One of our senior interviewees illustrates this point clearly:

> *'Lots of companies go wrong by implementing the IT-business relationship as a supplier-customer relationship. In these situations the business doesn't want or expect to be challenged by IT – they just want it to make stuff happen; but at the same time they complain that it doesn't add value. For IT to deliver real business value, the relationship between IT and business has to be more one of strategic partnership.'*

When an IT organisation is perceived as a supplier, or worse as a cost centre, the relationship between business and IT is fundamentally unbalanced. IT is subservient to the wishes of business. Of course it's unreasonable to expect IT people to be in charge, driving the business agenda and telling business department heads what to do, but there has to be a real partnership, or all sorts of problems can ensue.

'It takes two to tango'

One common symptom of 'subservient IT' is that business heads completely delegate responsibility for making IT decisions to the IT organisation and at the same time don't see the value of engaging with IT except when things go wrong.

Adam Overfield, managing director of Pure Power, explains:

> 'I've seen this in just about every organisation I've worked in: the Directors pay lip service to IT. They get somebody else to develop their IT strategy for them, it comes forward as a board paper, none of them read it and they sign it off and say "we'll adopt that as our strategy. Now you, Mr IT director/manager, you go and implement it, you deliver it to budget and to time". I've been in board meetings where that's actually what's happened. The IT manager has come forward with a glowing report saying he's achieved his budgets on time and on budget then the operations people have said, "this is rubbish, that's crap, this doesn't work, that doesn't work. . ." Then everybody sits back in their chairs and thinks: "well, what are we going to do now?"

Bob Doyle, former CIO of Kraft Foodservice, concurs:

> 'Many things get in the way of alignment and it's not always an IT issue – it takes two to tango, and the relationship between IT and business should be a partnership of equals. Many times, however, business looks to IT to solve problems and in many cases they're much too quick to offload thorny issues back to IT.'

The outcome is always that the IT organisation fails to deliver business value as far as the business is concerned, because fundamentally the business has said to the IT organisation: 'Oh, you know what we want, just sort it out.' But no CIO, senior IT manager or enterprise architect is a mind reader. To deliver business value, you have to be able to understand what the business values are.

IT is an afterthought

One of the executives we interviewed for this book – we'll not name them here – offered this beautifully succinct view relating to another symptom of subservient IT:

> *'Quite often a VP or similar will ask "why is IT in the room?" and the answer is that shit rolls downhill and it ends up with us. Seeing as your decisions are going to be impacting on us soon, we need to be here from the start to make sure it's done right.'*

Often, business needs to make quick decisions, and if IT is completely pigeonholed as a supplier, then when business executives decide to make changes to the way things work, the best thing that can happen is that technology gets dragged along behind. The shit rolls downhill, and the only thing that that the IT organisation can hope for is that it sees it coming in time. As a result, the business perceives IT as a ball-and-chain – holding business back – whereas from the IT side it seems that there is never enough forward visibility of planned changes.

Business and IT implementation projects are highly interdependent, but in most organisations it's unfortunately the case that the IT projects required for the successful implementation of business initiatives are afterthoughts. The trail of troublesome mergers and acquisitions, weakened by lack of thought about the IT implications, such as those between Lloyds Bank and TSB, and The Royal Bank of Scotland and National Westminster Bank, are testament to this.

Graeme Tozer, Principal Enterprise Architect, TUI United Kingdom, offers a nice example:

> *'As we do more EA work we're becoming more aware that in some cases IT has very little visibility of important changes coming along, except for at the very last minute. Decisions are made at board level, and as long as processes are followed the IT Director/CIO is involved. Occasionally, processes are not followed and the no-one is thinking about the IT implications. It's only when those initiatives get quite far advanced that anyone thinks about the IT issues.'*

It's a short step from a subservient, customer–supplier relationship dynamic like this to the wearyingly common lament within IT organisations: 'we spend all our IT budget fire-fighting, and we never have time to look at the more strategic issues.'

Efficient service provision brings short-term relief

It's enlightening that the traditional response to this challenge, espoused by technology vendors and technology consultants and advisors, has been to focus inwardly – on how IT operates – to see how 'keeping the lights on' can be made less expensive and resource draining, in order to make time and money available for dealing more strategic issues.

However, this is a myopic view that focuses, once more, on IT as a supplier. It's fine to try and make service provision more efficient – it's a laudable goal – but unless you work towards building a more equal partnership between IT and business, it's highly likely that the outcome of making IT service provision more efficient will be less than satisfying. You'll get a pat on the back for saving money, and you might get a bonus! But your IT budget for next year will most likely shrink in line with the savings you've engineered. Next year, you'll have the same challenges: only dealing with them will be even more difficult, because of the law of diminishing returns.

The implications of IT investment life cycles are ignored

Another dimension of the challenge of limited visibility of changes and their implications is that short-sightedness doesn't just reign in the consideration of new investments; it also reigns in the consideration of the implications of the life cycles of existing investments.

In particular, if there's no real partnership between IT and business at key touchpoints, to complement the 'foundation' supplier function from IT, ensuring that key systems have business owners can be a real challenge. IT has a long history of thinking a lot about how systems come to be built, and less so about how they're operated. Any transition on the IT side towards a more holistic consideration of the value of IT investments throughout their life cycles, without a similar shift on the business side, is of limited value. And that depends on the partnership between business and IT.

To put it concretely, one key way that this mismatch appears over and over again is that systems often outlive the initial context in which they were conceived, and the business-people who commissioned and sponsored the initial investment move on. When this happens, it's very difficult indeed for IT to find anyone on the business side willing to take responsibility for such a system going forward. 'It wasn't my idea,' they quite rightly say. . . but this is a classic symptom: ultimately, systems shouldn't be built because someone has a fancy that they should be; they should be built because there's a business need. If the business need is still there, someone in the business should be prepared to act as the 'business owner' of that system going forward.

As Richard Steel, the CIO at the London Borough of Newham, says:

> *'It's a major challenge: there's an erosion of ICT knowledge in businesses – the original commissioners of systems / services / processes move on, and succession planning is inadequate.'*

Out of sight is out of mind

It's common to see IT directors and CIOs in positions that are one, or even two, steps away from the management boards of large organisations. They might report to CFOs or COOs, or even commercial directors.

What's the reason for this level of disconnection? In a great many cases, it's a simple reflection of the fact that the CEO or MD is uncomfortable with IT. They don't understand it, they don't trust it or they don't see how it adds value. They don't see that actually there are multiple constituent parts to an IT organisation, which play distinct roles in delivering business value. So they give that part of the management portfolio to another executive officer to look after. Problem solved.

If you're reading this book, though, the chances are that you already realise that the overall role of IT in business is just too pervasive and multifaceted to have it squirreled away. The problem, indeed, again comes down to perception – typically where at least part of the IT capability is not managed into the CEO; it's because IT is seen as a cost centre – a drain on resources – or a simple service supplier.

Alignment imperatives

Given the challenges which arise from an unbalanced relationship between business and IT where IT is subservient to the desires of business, it should be clear that a fundamental reappraisal of the kind of relationship that exists between IT and business teams is in order.

Of course it's silly to expect that IT and business teams will be equal in every way, with IT executives, for example, telling business executives how to run things. The tail mustn't wag the dog. IT supports and should align with business needs, not the other way around.

But as we mentioned in Chapter 2, it's no longer acceptable for IT organisations to manage IT investments for their own sake. Neither is it acceptable to manage IT investments on behalf of the business. To create sustainable IT–business alignment, the baseline that we all have to aspire to is managing IT investments *within business*. But to do this effectively, we have to revisit the relationships that exist between IT and business, and look to fostering real partnerships between IT and business teams at all levels, in place of the supplier–customer relationships that are likely to exist today.

Achieving alignment

Put the CIO at the top

There might be a strong argument for a modular IT organisation – with 'brains' and 'brawn' separated. The 'foundation' service supplier function (the brawn) can feasibly report into a COO or operations director, if that is politically the right thing to do. But the other part of the IT organisation (the brain) – the part that works with the business – can't be considered in this way.

Why? Well, just as we explain in Chapter 6, justification for this reporting line comes from what's overwhelmingly likely to be scattered through the pages of the organisation's overall strategy. Look through the high-level strategy documents, and we'll bet that you'll find numerous examples of initiatives and directions that require cross-cutting change or investment programmes, heavily IT-dependent initiatives, and areas of rapid change or high risk that have major IT implications.

It's probably no surprise to you therefore that one of our key recommendations is that the CIO (or IT director) has to have a position at the top of the organisation, in the boardroom. After all, this is a popular view amongst consultancy and advisory firms.

It's tempting to brush this view off as the fancy of deep-thinking types with no experience of the real world, but it's surprising how consistently our research interviews highlighted this as a critical success factor in creating the right environment for sustainable IT–business alignment.

It transpires that there are two key reasons why it makes sound sense for the CIO to be sitting alongside the other key department heads, reporting into the CEO:

- First, as we've said time and again in this report, IT and business are intimately intertwined today, and there's unlikely to be a single business process in the organisation which isn't supported by IT. The constraints that business decisions place on how IT can deliver value, and the constraints that IT capabilities place on how business change can really happen, means that the IT organisation has to be involved in significant business decisions early.

- Secondly, and equally if not more importantly, the cross-organisational responsibility of the CIO means that they have the kind of horizontal view of the business that no other departmental head will have, with the possible exception of the CFO or financial director. Given the criticality of cross-organisational initiatives to so many of today's business strategies, the CIO therefore has an invaluable perspective.

Angela Yochem, a senior executive at one of the United States' largest banking organizations, corroborates this second point:

'Why does IT have to have a seat at the executive management table? There's real business value – the investment board gets a perspective from IT that's cross-cutting – and this perspective doesn't come from any of the other line-of-business types. In this respect IT is like finance – and you wouldn't think of not having someone from finance at that table.'

Bob Doyle, former CIO of Kraft Foodservice, makes his point even more forcefully:

'This is the most important of all the principles: the CIO has to be part of the strategic and executive planning process. If you're not in that place you can't know what's going on – and that's from both strategic and operational perspectives. If the CIO is part of the process, they can see the difference between what needs to be done and what the business says needs to be done – and they also get to know at the right time.
If the CIO can't gain access to the executive table, there are major limitations to what can be done to align IT and business. The relationship will always be unequal, business will always make unreasonable demands, and the strategic value of IT will always be under-delivered.'

Richard Steel, CIO of the London Borough of Newham, further illustrates the second reason for putting the CIO at the top of the organisation:

'Why is it so important that the IT organisation is represented at a very senior level? Principally because of service and business integration trends. In order to serve the business properly in this environment, the argument that "the IT organisation can only be an infrastructure provider" falls over, because delivery of integrated services means that the IT organisation has to provide and promote consistency of systems and information across projects and programmes, in order to get maximum business value from IT.'

The problem is that if the IT organisation isn't able to report directly to the CEO, then whichever department or function the IT organisation reports into, its energies and budgets will be directed disproportionately to focus on that area.

We talked recently to a senior IT manager at a UK energy utility, where the IT organisation was managed under the customer services department. Despite the fact that IT management could see a number of opportunities to help reduce cost and enable innovation in other areas of the business, they had a hard time getting sign-off for any activity that didn't in some way contribute to the operation of the customer services function.

Another interviewee recounted the history of how the IT organisation at a European airline was affected by reporting line changes:

> *'For a long time the IT–business relationship was mature and effective. There had been a significant "partnership and reorientation exercise" between business and IT, and we'd managed to drive some cross-departmental initiatives, working across silos in both IT and business, and IT was seen as strategic. However when we got a new CEO, he put IT under the Engineering Director, and things went downhill. We started to be managed like an engineering departments. Luckily, a couple of years later, when another new CEO was drafted in, he brought IT back out and appointed a CIO – and things started to improve again.'*

Make the business accountable

Below the top level of IT and business management, the peer relationship between IT and business needs to continue to operate when it comes to the pursuit of individual IT change or investment programmes and projects.

Historically some organisations have managed to consistently engage project sponsors from the business in actively working to define and refine the project scope, terms of reference and requirements; but there's more to it than that as Bob Doyle, former CIO of Kraft Foodservice, points out:

> *'The CIO has to have a place at the top table, but success can't come from the CIO "going it alone": there has to be a lead business executive involved in every large IT effort, who is held jointly accountable for the project with the CIO. To maximise the effectiveness of this approach, use this kind of partnership to create a joint steering group for the project which brings in personnel from "both sides".'*

For example if you're asked to do a big ERP implementation that crosses multiple departments, be prepared to say 'no' – unless you get business representation on the project. Big initiatives like this aren't IT projects; they're business transformation projects, and without active senior business involvement in projects like these, they will lose momentum very quickly.

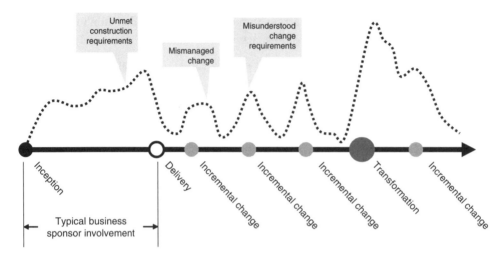

Figure 5.1: Risks through the IT investment life cycle

As we highlighted above, business ownership of and participation in major IT projects have to extend past the initial design and development of systems. Most major IT projects yield systems that last 5 years or more – or even decades. Shared responsibility is, in the end, a good thing because it helps to manage risk, but given the extended lifetimes of a great many systems and the persistence of business change, it's folly to assume that the business and IT risks associated with systems disappear once those systems are deployed. As Figure 5.1 shows, this is a long way from the truth. The risks are different later in the life cycle of an IT investment, but they don't stop impinging on the delivery of value from IT capabilities.

This means that business participation has to be there not only when investments are first made but throughout the lifetimes of the systems that arise from those investments.

John Johnson, CIO of Intel, provides a concrete example:

'One of the most strategic parts of our IT landscape is our SAP system. Over the years, it has got out of line with business requirements, because of the architectural foundation for the original implementation. This meant it was difficult to keep things aligned as business processes involved. So, we were in a position of having a 10-year-old system that was inflexible, difficult to extend and no longer supported by the original supplier.

The only thing to do was sit down with the CEO, the CFO and key business managers and talk through our options. This was very much a partnership style discussion as what was on the table was a complete re-engineering of not just a system that was core to our business, but also many of the business processes it supported. To pull this one off, there was a need for both the IT function and the various parts of the business to understand that it would only work if there was a genuine joint effort, with everyone pulling together in the same direction with clear motives and a clear set of priorities. For example, there would obviously be a lot of IT resource involved, but also we would need the time of key people from the business.'

Effective IT leaders can't afford to hope that business leaders will take up the challenge: they have too much else to do and it's easy to duck responsibility. Effective IT leaders have to actively pursue business leaders to make commitments. Darin Brumby, CIO of First Group, is adamant that business leaders have to be coerced into making decisions, because putting decisions off causes so many problems:

'Apathy and status quo are killers. You have to do the right thing: look at someone directly in the eye and say, this is unacceptable, it isn't good enough that you aren't making a decision. I pointed out these risks, and I didn't do it just to give you an update. You need to take a decision on one, two, three of them. A non-decision doesn't cut it.'

Embed IT people in business operations

In an ideal world, where IT was really just infrastructure with a load of knobs on which the business could tweak, organisations could live with a state of affairs where the IT organisation was merely a straightforward supplier of services which complied with requirements. But the reality, as we all know, is that the role that IT plays within business represents something very far from this mechanistic, deterministic utopia. IT footprints place constraints on what business can do, and business cultures and organisational patterns place constraints on what IT can do. So although one of overall roles of the IT organisation is that of a supplier, there has to be more to it than that. The 'more' is a set of teams embedded in the business that have reporting lines into the IT organisation, but that work day-to-day with operational business issues.

As we've said above it's critical to get commitment from businesspeople to take ownership of IT investments throughout their life cycles. However, with the best will in the world, it's unreasonable to expect businesspeople to proactively work in this kind of arrangement, because there's too much else for them to do. Consequently, the IT organisation has to maintain business engagement, by working actively within the business.

Of course, IT organisations have worked with the business since the days when the 'waterfall' software development methodology reigned supreme. Since time immemorial, it seems, business-savvy (or at least, not too antisocial) IT people would be trained to do requirements analysis work, and at the start of every software development project, these 'business analysts' would set up meetings with groups of 'users' and elicit requirements through a series of interview sessions. However, at the end of the business analysis phase of the project, these people would disappear; the big heavy doors to the IT temple would shut and everything would go quiet. Every so often a 'user' would stray close to the temple and hear the banging of anvils and occasional swearing. Then, after many months of silence (interspersed with anvil banging and swearing), the doors to the temple would grandly swing open, and the system would be wheeled out. 'Hmm,' the users would say, 'that wasn't really what I was after. . .'

This intermittent interaction just isn't enough. No, what's needed for is a subset of the IT organisation's staff to be embedded in business teams working side by side with business-people, understanding what they do, engaging them in conversations and hearing their feedback. These IT people need to have a significant degree of authority to prioritise changes and enhancements to systems. They cannot just be embedded when software development projects are being delivered, or when systems are first rolled out: they're embedded for the lifetime of the systems.

Jon Larsen, IT Project Director, Dresdner Kleinwort, explains:

> '*It is more difficult for the IT organisation to talk directly to the business, as opposed to hiding behind the technology. IT personnel are paid an element to be differentiating and, as a result, must be out there engaging with the business rather than in the comfort zone of technology. The IT organisation must see IT in operation in the business e.g. by sitting on the trading floor and understanding what is really happening.*'

Service managers – a crucial relationship management role

Although they will sit outside the core IT service delivery organisation, these people can be thought of as 'service managers'. They act as bridges between the consumers of services and the service provider – or service providers. Indeed, it's likely that an internal IT organisation will act as only one service provider among many (something we discuss more in Chapter 8), and in this context, individuals playing service management roles are acting as both relationship managers, interfacing between the business and the IT service providers, and service brokers, interfacing with external service providers. As shown in Figure 5.2, this key job role has several elements, which mirror many aspects of product management and customer service management disciplines:

- aggregating service demand information and feedback from service consumers in the business

- filtering and funnelling this information back to service provider(s) as necessary

- filtering and funnelling this information back to the enterprise architecture (see Chapter 4) and ITGB (see Chapter 6) teams, when the need for investment decisions becomes apparent

- helping facilitate project management conversations between business teams, enterprise architects and IT project delivery teams

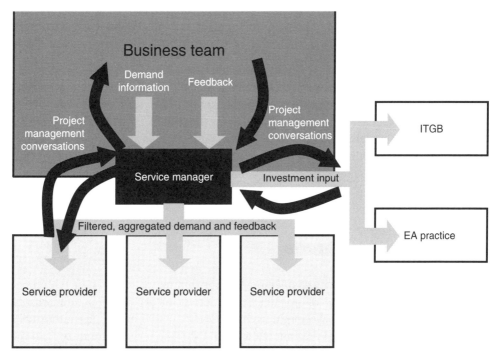

Figure 5.2: Service managers – relationship managers and service brokers

Richard Steel explains the way that he's put this service management role to work in his organisation:

'The challenge we have had, is that although individual users had the highest priority in terms of day-to-day IT activity, they had the lowest level of influence in terms of the direction we took. Historically, an "IT strategy board" was put together from the user community to help drive our direction, but this proved not to be effective over time: the members weren't really "living IT" but rather only thought about it at board meetings.

> *So we instigated what I call a "portfolio management" approach. This involves "portfolio managers", each of whom manages a set of IT services, sitting day-to-day in the service units where the customers work. They have end-to-end lifecycle responsibility for their IT services, and they spend their time championing business concerns to IT, and vice versa. Portfolio managers are expected to sit on the management teams of the organisations they're placed with.'*

What's particularly interesting is how individuals were developed into this role. Richard hired some external mentors and then used them to identify IT employees with the right skills and motivations and train them up to take on the role. Interestingly it wasn't always the existing business analysts who made the grade.

Another way in which service managers can really add value to the IT organisation is by identifying new ways for IT to support existing business practice, or even by identifying ways for IT to enable new and innovative business practice. A core IT service provider organisation is a great vehicle for 'getting the basics right', but it's not set up to really drive innovation – either within IT or within the business more broadly. Service managers can provide that layer of real added value, if they have the appropriate authority and responsibility.

Adopt the right attitude

Although we've focused in this chapter on the positioning of key IT staff within the broader organisation, our research for this book and our history of interactions with IT executives through the years have taught us that it doesn't matter how much authority IT people have in the wider organisation, if they don't discharge their authority with the right attitude.

Effective communication between business and IT demands that IT professionals step up to the plate. If you're implementing the other principles described in this book, you're likely to be in a position where IT is starting to be trusted and respected. The 'last mile' is to make sure that representatives of the IT organisation behave in a way that reflects and supports the partnership nature of the IT–business relationship that you're looking to nurture.

Every IT representative in a role which involves significant interactions with business teams has to take responsibility for positioning IT as more than a cost centre, and more than a passive service provider. Enterprise architects and service managers in particular must be the kind of people who don't just accept what they're told, but instead question – asking why the business is interested in a particular feature, why things are done a certain way and, where necessary, pushing back against impractical ideas and suggestions.

As Nick Malik of Microsoft says:

> *'The problem is that IT people are trained to be service providers – to take direction – and say "ok, we understand your requirement, we'll build it and it'll be good". What they need to be trained to do is say: "Are you sure? Well OK, this is how it's got to be – you can't have exactly what you want because it'll screw up 8 other things that are strategically important. But we can do it this *other* way, and you'll get a lot of what you want without causing problems for everybody else."'*

If you're the sort of individual capable of doing this, you should not be afraid, or see it as sign of weakness, to ask questions. Questioning is the most effective route to developing effective relationships. It would be all too easy to initiate the conversation along the lines of 'I'm from IT and I'm here to help', but that is going to be met with a good deal of justified scepticism. Instead, service managers and enterprise architects must be prepared to step back, observe and engage with businesspeople on their terms, based on a genuine interest in what the business does.

As we discussed in Chapter 4, they must be comfortable focussing on what the business needs to achieve – and what is getting in the way – and only then explain how IT can help. How they communicate is just as important as what they communicate. They should not be engaging in a conversation which assumes, for reasons we have already discussed, a supplier–customer relationship. Instead, they should be prepared to become part of the team or – as Richard Steel put it, champions for the business, even if that challenges their relationships with their IT peers.

Maintaining alignment

Develop networking and people skills

One of the most fundamental challenges standing in the way of building and maintaining peer relationships between business and IT folks is that, as we've signposted in a number of places, many IT staff, particularly technologists, aren't comfortable in business scenarios – where in many cases it's not about what you know; it's about who you know. Networking and persuasion are key skills that every good businessperson has in his or her armoury, but if you think of the average software architect, these things just aren't on their radar.

As Richard Steel, CIO of the London Borough of Newham, highlights, IT managers can suffer from the same challenges:

> *'Many IT managers are introverts. It's important to develop your networking and selling skills if you're going to succeed in working alongside senior business managers. Even if you're not comfortable doing it, look for opportunities to do public speaking, go to networking events, join industry bodies and get actively involved. This will also help raise your visibility and improve your standing in the eyes of other senior business managers.'*

Nick Malik of Microsoft confirms that networking skills are vital in large organisations:

> *'To be effective you have to really know the organisation. To persuade the really influential people you have to have lunch with them before you need to ask them a favour. You need to know the name of their cat, if that's important to them. You have to know what motivates them, and they need to know what motivates you. So networking is an incredibly important part of what it takes to be effective.'*

Bob Doyle remarks:

> *'A key contributor to an unequal relationship is a lack of skills on the IT side – particularly good programme and project management and associated skills, and effective communication skills.'*

These three strong voices are part of a much larger chorus of senior IT staff which consistently calls out the importance of networking and people skills to overall IT–business alignment. Of course, it's silly to expect all IT staff to go on a 'people skills training course', but there are key roles in every IT organisation which must be filled by personnel who have these skills. Service managers, enterprise architects, IT managers/ CIOs, programme managers and project managers stand out as prime targets.

Plan for succession

Succession planning is vital to ensuring sustainable IT–business alignment. But what do we mean by this?

It comes down to a simple fact. In a great many cases, business-critical systems and the services they provide outlive the executives that initially sponsored their creation, the procurement team that drew up the supplier contracts, the developers that customised, built or integrated the solution, and other important stakeholders.

Of course, sound software engineering principles – properly documented requirements, designs, deployment guides and operational procedures, all linked in the context of business needs – help enormously from the perspective of succession planning on the IT side. However, even these things, which are the established IT best practices, rarely get done consistently. And with the advent of agile software development, there's a worrying swing in some quarters (primarily where people accidentally or intentionally misunderstand the discipline associated with agile development) towards these things being considered less and less important.

IT succession planning aside, there remains the problem of succession planning from the business perspective. As we mentioned above, if there's still a business need for a service to be delivered, then there should be a business executive willing to step up to the plate and take a degree of joint ownership (with a service manager, probably) of the service being provided.

Things like this don't happen by accident, of course. You have to manage the organisation with these goals in mind. You need to define and enforce management policies, from the top of the organisation down, that steer an orderly and appropriate handover of responsibilities for IT services as business executives transition in and out of the organisation.

This management call to action is in fact an extension of putting your own house in order that we highlighted in Chapter 3. You don't only need to be able to manage and assure capabilities in terms of technology infrastructure and people skills and resources for managing that infrastructure; what we're talking about here is the need to manage and assure IT and business capabilities that can deliver sustainable service change management.

Summary

- It can be very tempting to work to create a supplier–consumer relationship between the IT organisation and business teams, with business teams acting as 'customers' whose requirements are fulfilled by IT. It's perhaps a logical conclusion of the desire to 'run IT like a business'. But this is only a partial view and can only take you so far in really creating sustainable IT–business alignment, because suppliers are by their very nature subservient: they do what they're told. There is a place for this, in the 'vanilla' delivery of services to support business needs, but there is another factor in the alignment equation that is less about 'doing things right' (the focus of service delivery) and more about 'doing the right thing'. This key aspect of alignment can't be fulfilled by an IT organisation acting as a passive supplier.

- There are two primary aspects where the peer relationship must be worked on: at the strategic level, between the CIO and the board; and at the operational level, between business teams and IT staff responsible for day-to-day service and project delivery.

- It's very difficult to create a peer relationship between IT and business without the CIO in a position at the top of the organisation. There is real value in this arrangement: not least, in most large organisations the CIO is one of only a very small number of executives with the kind of end-to-end, cross-cutting view of the organisation as a whole that is so important to the fulfilment of today's business strategies.

- Real peer relationships must be developed with commitment from both IT and business executives, and their scope must encompass more than discrete IT projects (which is what such relationships typically focus on where they do exist today). Two-way dialogues between IT and business executives are important because they're a great assistant in the management of risk, but risks don't go away once systems are deployed. Systems often live for many years or even decades, and risks associated with changes (both planned and environmental) need to be managed for long after the initial system deployment.

- Sustainable relationships between IT and business executives will only come when the notion of real engagement between IT and business becomes internalised as part of the culture within both IT and business. Succession planning on both sides of the house is particularly important, and on the IT side, networking and people skills are likely to need urgent attention. Service managers, enterprise architects, IT managers/CIOs, programme managers and project managers stand out as prime targets.

6

Work towards coordinated goals and objectives

Building a common language which is shared between business and IT staff is a fantastic achievement – but by itself it won't create the kind of environment required to support sustainable IT–business alignment.

Why? Because, as our research has highlighted, one of the key impediments to IT–business alignment is the lack of coordination and shared vision between business units and departments. It's all very well for IT and business practitioners to understand each other tactically, but we need more than a common language if ever-broadening communities of IT stakeholders – people with very different motivations – are to communicate in a way that promotes agreement on what's important and what isn't. A shared language clearly helps here – as does having the CIO in a board role at the top of the organisation as we discuss elsewhere – but you also need to foster a culture and organisation that promotes working together in a coordinated way to meet shared goals and objectives.

Common areas of misalignment

> '*The challenge ... is about telling someone that in order to make things better, they have to spend a bit more up front – and that extra spend will end up making *other* people's lives easier. Doing this is a bit like saying, "You're the first person to want to drive between Kansas and New York, so you're going to need to pay to have all the bridges built on the route." The client says, "No way." How do you persuade them?"*'
>
> Nick Malik, Enterprise Architect, Microsoft

Interwoven IT creates many side-effects

As we explained earlier in this book, a key part of the alignment imperative that exists in organisations throughout the world today comes from the fact that business today is saturated with IT. IT is now woven into the very fabric of business, but unfortunately, the ways in which IT organisations and business teams work together doesn't always reflect this.

As the Figure 6.1 below illustrates, the level of 'IT saturation' that now exists within organisations means that as new business initiatives start to be implemented and as

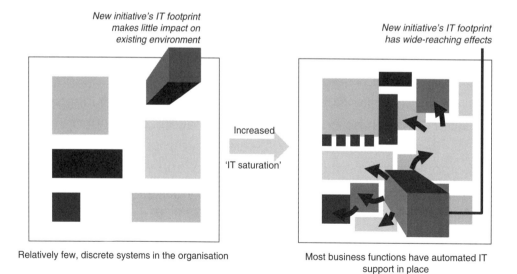

New initiative's IT footprint makes little impact on existing environment

New initiative's IT footprint has wide-reaching effects

Increased

'IT saturation'

Relatively few, discrete systems in the organisation

Most business functions have automated IT support in place

Figure 6.1: Less IT whitespace means more side-effects

IT systems are deployed to support them, cascades of consequences are often unavoidable.

Directly or indirectly, information technology creates connections within and between businesses where they haven't existed before (we used the word 'woven' on purpose). There aren't many business projects or ideas these days where the results are nicely contained in a neat organisational box. More and more, the requirement to use IT to support a business initiative creates effects that are (or which should be) felt far outside the initiative's initial scope.

Let's consider a hypothetical initiative taken by a mobile phone network operator (let's call it Purplenet) to outsource a product support call centre as an example.

In order to track and improve product quality for future development work, the call centre needs a system which allows operatives to record the details of enquiries, as well as ensuring that only licensed Purplenet customers can receive product support. So a new system is deployed in the offshore location, and a subset of the customer database is imported. To ensure that the two customer lists are kept synchronised, Purplenet's HQ batches up new customer details and forwards them to the offshore operation weekly.

A few months later there's an urgent need to reconsider things, for two reasons: first of all, Purplenet's customer support manager has noticed that 5% (and growing) of free support calls are logged by people who have actually not renewed their premium support contracts. Secondly, the company's biggest competitor, H2O, has improved its service commitment to customers: with H2O, your phone will work within 10 minutes of you having bought it. Purplenet's CEO wants to match this commitment.

The first problem has arisen because the mechanism for removing customer details from the offshore call centre's systems hasn't been properly implemented. No one thought of telling HQ's business systems development manager that this was of high priority and she wasn't part of the original team that worked on the outsourcing project. She tried to keep up with the goings-on in the outsourcing project by catching up on gossip from colleagues, but another project – the current pet project of the VP for revenue management – was keeping her team working all hours.

Secondly, with the current arrangement in place, Purplenet can't make the kind of commitment that H2O is making to its customers because new customers might have to wait a week before the support call centre will allow them to log an enquiry.

Now, it's clear, the offshore call centre and HQ's business systems need to have a much more intimate level of integration that allows customer information to be updated back and forth very quickly. The question is – who's going to pay for the infrastructure required?

The broad scope of the (quite often unexpected or unintended) effects that spring from IT-enabled business initiatives presents a real challenge because the ways in which most organisations are structured and managed – and the cultures which have grown to reinforce those structures and management approaches – tend to work in a way that ignores the interconnectedness of business activities, promoted by interconnected IT, that is inherent 'on the ground'.

Business teams are optimised for laser focus on their own operational performance

As we discuss in Chapter 4, business departments and IT teams alike are specialised things. They've got this way because in many cases specialisation is vital to success. Business teams have specialised skills in finance, purchasing or marketing for example, whereas technology teams have specialised skills in database administration or Java software development. But when specialised teams become firm organisational units, they also become budget holders. And along with that they take on profit-and-loss responsibility, and their managers become focused on driving for optimum performance in their own area.

Of course, this isn't normally a problem – but when business functions pursue their own financial performance to the exclusion of broader considerations, that's when the problems start.

Andreas Dietrich, CIO of SBB, is working hard to counter this tendency to focus narrowly within business units. He explains:

> '*The SBB business units are extremely driven by day-to-day questions and not by strategic considerations – i.e. where the business will be in 2-3 years. This is a big challenge. We have to move away from a project-based view of working and communicating with the business and toward a more strategic and portfolio-based view of the business over the coming 2-3 years.*
>
> *The underlying problem I see in industry is that most business management incentives don't reward the right business behaviours. Managers are rewarded for driving profit and loss in their area exclusively, rather than on driving collaborative/shared projects and thinking.*'

In many large organisations there's a real culture of competition between divisions and departments. Sometimes this culture yields high performance results – but increasingly, because important business initiatives have 'IT footprints' that spread out across reporting structures, it's vital to find ways to temper this inter-departmental competitive spirit.

Darin Brumby, CIO of First Group, has experienced this first-hand:

'We created the First shared services structure to deliver IT services across all the global businesses, each of which is a billion dollar businesses in its own right. I remember a year and a half in, when one of my team's bosses was saying, "we're really going great guns here, none of the other functions are anywhere near us".... I said, "that's the problem. It's no good if the other functions stay half-divisionalised in some impeded organisational structure that doesn't actually get the work done that makes the money. We need to drag them along with us. Our success isn't about how far ahead we are of everybody else in the organisation: it's about how well we pull them with us."

It's far better to create a culture in which you can just bring these people on that journey so that you might change the thinking, and the potential for sustainability, and move the company to be a great company.'

Laser focus and tunnel vision

The problem with a laser focus on operational performance is that one man's laser focus is another man's tunnel vision. A common symptom of the tunnel vision that many business teams exhibit in their operation is the 'pet project'.

Although at a high level IT and business teams may agree on a set of plans and have a shared understanding about key concepts and critical priorities, it's typically the case that on the ground, the budget holders in business divisions continue to fund projects that they have a personal interest in pursuing. Often this is because they have a strongly held belief that the project will enable them to do something out of the ordinary and reap them financial rewards and kudos. Other times, it's because they've been convinced by a technologist that a particular kind of IT investment will solve a major pain point (whereas the truth might be that the technologist wants the opportunity to advance their CV, rather than the company's success).

An IT Director for a leading global financial services firm (who's requested to remain anonymous) spells it out:

'There are situations where projects that should be funded to support key business initiatives are not being funded, because of budget issues and 'pet projects' receiving funding... we've created business and technology road maps which are in the process of being aligned, but the allocation of budgets to projects is another dimension which is currently not effectively aligned with those road maps.'

IT strategy work is disjointed and disconnected

In the 1980s and 1990s, a dominant IT project methodology, James Martin and Clive Finkelstein's Information Engineering, advocated an initial step focused on 'Information Strategy Planning':

'Information strategy planning is primarily concerned with the organization as a whole, its business goals and critical success factors. It also deals with opportunities and competitive advantages that companies can realise through technology. The result of the planning process builds a high-level view of the organization, its business functions, its geographic distribution and its information needs.'

This is a laudable aim and should create real value. However, Information Engineering's approach to strategy work – that it is the first stage of discrete IT development projects rather than a separate and ongoing process – remains embedded in the cultures of many IT departments in large organisations, despite the fact that Information Engineering has fallen out of favour in many large organisations as a development project methodology.

As a result much IT strategy work is *disjointed* (there are few common threads pulling occasional bursts of strategy definition work together) and *disconnected* (IT strategy work uses business context as an input, but its output is purely directed at optimising IT solutions). We discuss how to remedy some of the limitations of these approaches to strategy work in Chapter 5.

A drive to restructure IT footprints

As our fictional Purplenet example illustrated, a great many organisations are in a position where, from a management perspective at least, they've stumbled accidentally into a world where integration and coordination of existing IT investments and platforms is the major issue in the implementation of new business initiatives.

In IT management circles there's now a growing realisation that technology integration is something that has to be considered as a systemic property, so that organisations move towards an intentional, rather than an accidental, approach to integration – as Figure 6.2 below illustrates.

However, there's a significant gap between this and the level of understanding of the issue in the broader business management community. And moreover, there are relatively few signs that organisations are really taking up the challenge.

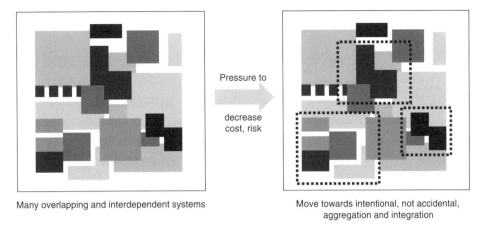

Pressure to

decrease
cost, risk

Many overlapping and interdependent systems

Move towards intentional, not accidental,
aggregation and integration

Figure 6.2: Side-effects drive pressure to restructure

One piece of evidence for this comes from a 2006 survey of IT executives at large UK organisations:

Less than half of those firms surveyed had specific teams assigned to integration projects, while only 38 percent undertook 'proof of concept' practices prior to integration projects. Forty-five percent of firms undertook integration projects on a case-by-case basis, and over half made purchasing decisions for each individual project rather than using a standard enterprise-wide set of tools that are part of an existing development environment. [Intersystems/PMP Study]

There's significant industry interest in Service Oriented Architecture (SOA) as a potential method of harmonising approaches to IT system integration. However, as shown in a research study we carried out in 2006 and highlighted in Figure 6.3 below, the truth is that for most organisations the end-to-end use of a single unified approach to structuring the IT footprints of business initiatives remains an aspiration. While Enterprise Application Integration (EAI) technology, which first became popular in the mid-1990s, was supposed to do precisely this, a great many organisations find themselves struggling under the weight of multiple different EAI investments, not least because they were pursued in exactly the same way as the initiatives they set out to integrate – to support the needs of particular business functions.

Alignment imperatives

Given how important it is to drive towards restructuring the IT footprints that business initiatives create, and given the problems that today's organisational structures and cultures create, it should be clear that although having a common IT and business language and your

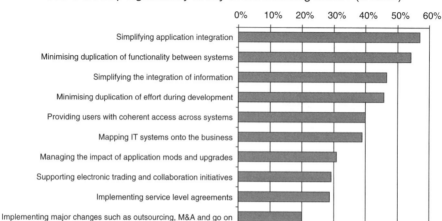

Figure 6.3: SOA is seen as a way to harmonise approaches to IT integration
Source: **Freefrom Dynamics/Macehiter Ward-Dutton** *SOA Perceptions & Practicalities* **study (conducted on behalf of IBM) in May/june 2006**[1]

CIO in a senior position are necessary for sustainable IT–business alignment, they aren't by themselves sufficient. It's not enough for IT and business to agree at the most senior levels; business groups need to agree between themselves on shared priorities in terms of how they will work with IT, and they can't do this without external help.

Truly sustainable IT–business alignment can only come from a combination of the right kind of organisation (an organisation which promotes peer relationships between business and IT), the right kind of language (a shared language which can be understood by business and IT) and the *right approach to getting things done*. Organisation and language get you to the starting blocks, but only through practical processes will you be able to run the race.

So what are the main aspects of these practical processes you need to put in place?

Achieving alignment

Define a cascade of shared commitments

In the spirit of not attempting to 'boil the ocean' when drawing up the scope for a process which will help foster shared goals across IT and business teams, it's tempting to focus efforts on securing commitments only at the highest levels – both in terms of stakeholders

---

[1]Online study of 1332, predominantly IT, professionals from a cross-section of industries, geographies and organisation sizes

(focusing on working with senior managers) and in terms of activity (focusing on agreeing high-level statements of direction and similar things).

It's great to be able to say, for example, 'we've achieved buy-in from all senior VPs on our core divisional strategies'.

The problem with this, especially in large organisations, is that this kind of buy-in is unlikely to have very much practical impact on the way IT and business teams work together day-to-day.

Real, practical forward movement will only come as this work expands to cover shared understanding of and commitment to goals at lower levels of the organisation (middle-level business managers, senior IT architects and so on) and finer-grained activities (individual initiatives, programmes and projects).

Vital to this is a broader perspective on the types of commitment that IT and business teams have to come to share between them. Commitments not only have to be made at the highest level, but they also have to have relevance in the day-to-day direction of IT work. We expand on this below.

Figure 6.4 below provides an overview of the key types of information or document that should really be part of the scope of your work here and how they inter-relate.

This 'cascade of shared commitments' mirrors the core of the common language that you should work to inculcate in the minds of all key IT and business representatives and is discussed in more detail in Chapter 9.

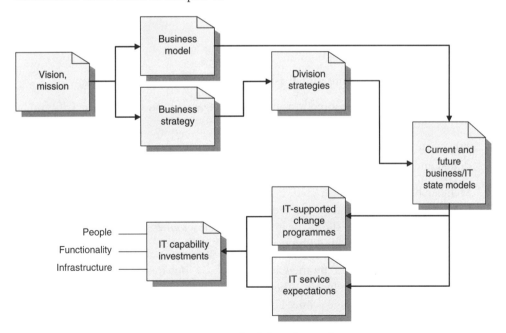

Figure 6.4: A cascade of shared commitments

Establish an IT Governance Board with teeth

The critical first step in creating shared commitment between IT and business groups – and between individual business groups in terms of their relationships with the IT organisation – is to uncover the business and IT road maps that different groups work to do.

These road maps should be derived from the 'current and future business/IT state models' illustrated in Figure 6.4 above, and should define paths that will take the organisation from the 'as-is' state to the 'to-be' state of both business and IT. Critically, the road maps should ensure consistency between the IT and business sides of the equation. These road maps are central to effective alignment, so they must be 'under management' in a clearly defined place. This means creating a forum in which they are published, shared, synchronised and in which changes to them are transparently managed. We call this forum the 'IT Governance Board' (ITGB).

In our work with organisations over the years, we've frequently found that there is no such forum. There is no individual or identified team which knows where all business and IT road maps are maintained and by whom. In some cases, it even becomes clear that little is actually written down *anywhere*, let alone in one place. Strategies and road maps aren't formalised, but they only exist in managers' heads. (Obviously, if yours is an organisation such as this, you have a lot of work to do. Read Chapter 5 for guidance on how you can get started.)

There are two key aspects to defining the ITGB: organisation and process.

Organisational aspects

There are a number of organisational aspects to defining the ITGB:

- The ITGB has to be sponsored by top-level management (and ideally, the CIO will be part of this group)

- The ITGB must be the one and only forum where strategy and road map work are shared and socialised across IT and business teams

- Membership should be restricted. Permanent members should include the CIO, the CEO, the CFO and the CTO (if there is one). Other executives (the head of sales and marketing, for example) should be invited to meetings when relevant – but when they are invited, attendance should be mandatory

- The ITGB can be 'owned' by the CIO or the CEO, but there has to be a very good reason for it to be owned by any other board-level executive. Certainly it shouldn't be owned by the CTO, if there is one. The ITGB's work isn't about technology strategy – it's about marrying business initiatives to IT capabilities. Under no circumstances should ownership of the ITGB be delegated to middle management

- Costs of operating the ITGB (principally executives' time, but possibly including external consulting fees) can be borne within the CEO's strategy budget or the CIO's budget, but its costs shouldn't be absorbed into the day-to-day operational IT budget.

Ensure an open process

In order to truly foster an agreement on goals and objectives across fiefdoms in large organisations, the ITGB investment review process has to secure reasoned feedback from all the stakeholders who have an interest in the proposed investment in question (whether they're directly proposing an investment or the investment has the potential to add or erode value in their area).

For example, a proposed investment in a technology capability to develop a single, harmonised view of customer information might be proposed by the VP of Marketing, or by the CIO. They should provide input to the review process, of course, but so should every other senior business executive with an interest in having access to good quality customer information (hint: that should be most of them).

Detailed technical input or feedback is not necessary or desirable; however, financial input – overviews of estimated costs and benefits – is. The goal of this review process is to get a high-level handle on how well aligned with the business goals and strategy a proposed investment might be. The kind of information that is useful to collect is illustrated in the sample stakeholder feedback scorecard shown in Figure 6.5 below.

Specifically, the investment review process should work towards the following outcomes:

- All the stakeholders in every proposed investment are clearly identified

- All the stakeholders know that they are stakeholders and as such will be called upon if the investment goes ahead to provide input and feedback to delivery programmes

Description	Type	Importance	Fit	Alignment	Risks
Short description of the proposed investment, including costs and benefits	[N]ew, [C]hange, [R]etain	How important is this to the stakeholder? [0 -10]	How well does the investment fit with what stakeholder wants? [0 -10]	Does this recommendation fit with strategies as stated?	If alignment is poor, what are the risks and why should we bear them? How can we minimise them?

Figure 6.5: A sample stakeholder feedback scorecard

- All stakeholders agree on a common investment priority list.

Where an organisation has a number of discrete IT budgets and autonomous departmental IT organisations under the control of individual business leaders, in addition to a central IT organisation, this structure has to be respected while at the same time ensuring that IT–business alignment overall is sustained.

'Private' investments – playing the Joker

One way to do this is to allow individual business leaders to 'play a Joker card' in the investment review process, which enables them to opt out of having their proposed investments vetoed by other line-of-business executives. Regardless of them opting out of formal investment review by their peers or by the CIO however, they should still fill out a scorecard to highlight whether (and to what degree) this 'private' investment will contribute towards overall IT–business alignment. If a positive alignment contribution can't be demonstrated, then the CEO or CIO should still be able to veto the investment or require proposal rework.

However it's important to legislate for the issues that commonly arise in these kinds of organisational situation, where departmental IT groups make investments without scrutiny, which nevertheless turn out to have an impact on central IT provision. Indeed this is ever more likely as organisations' business real estate gets more and more crowded with overlapping IT systems. So if a 'private investment' has implications for a shared IT organisation and the capabilities that it provides, these implications must be explicitly represented in a separate investment proposal that follows the 'normal' review rules. To ensure that these dependencies are properly uncovered in advance of private investments being made, it's vital that stakeholders in central IT groups (principally the CIO) get to review private investment proposals.

Many large organisations with long histories of working with IT operate in precisely the kind of environment that warrants this kind of smart investment review process. As the IT director of a major financial institution (who's requested to remain anonymous) explains:

'Another challenge for a huge multi-national such as us is that different businesses are optimised in different ways: the capital markets group and its IT model are very different from the consumer banking group. The former is optimised for flexibility and agility since it has higher margins and wants to be at the cutting edge, offering new services; whilst the latter is optimised for efficiency, reflecting the fact that it is operating on very tight margins and cost-per-transaction is everything. The consumer banking group wants to drive standard processes and procedures to drive out cost,

> *whilst the capital markets group is more interested in time-to-market for new products and services. These differences in priorities and technology need are in part the reason for the split of shared services between business and core IT, since it is challenging for shared services to balance the needs for agility and efficiency.'*

Organisations don't get much larger than Intel. John Johnson, the CIO, corroborated the above anecdote when we asked him how potential conflicts are managed between business units and their views of IT investment priorities:

> *'That is a very good question and it goes back to the governance model we are putting into place, which involves setting overall priorities from the CEO level downwards. If overall alignment of priorities between IT and the business is not defined at this level, then you will always have a battle on your hands. Conflicts obviously arise from time to time, mostly at middle management layer, but because of the top down prioritisation model we have in place, they quickly get resolved when general managers pick up the phone to each other. Again, a lot of this is about effective communication between the right people at the right level.'*

Bottom-up, as well as top-down governance input

If you're serious about IT being able to act as a force from innovation, as well as being an organisation dedicated to ensuring process efficiency and effectiveness, then the investment review process of the ITGB can't just be driven top-down – it's got to be possible for a 'junior' staff member to propose investment ideas and have them considered by the ITGB.

If this is to work in a manageable way, what's crucial is that good candidates for investment ideas get properly sponsored. This sponsorship is both for a senior executive taking an investment idea to the ITGB and presenting it on behalf of the originator, and also for ensuring that beforehand, the idea originator has sufficient assistance in developing and explaining the idea in the context of how the ITGB looks at the world (i.e., through the scorecard we illustrated in Figure 6.5).

This places responsibilities on senior executive members of the ITGB to act as incubators for investment ideas that come from their staff – helping the originators of ideas to understand the concept of IT–business alignment and how they can better express and refine their ideas so that they fit with the organisation's strategies and road maps.

Build a 'straw man' action plan

Regardless of whether business and IT strategies and road maps are in existence, it's important to ensure that they are properly joined up in a way that supports the common language you're creating to be shared by IT and business teams as their terms of reference.

This is quite unlikely to have been done before, and in the spirit of being a proactive leader (*see* Chapter 5 for more detail), it makes sense for you and your team to take the initiative and create a 'straw man' action plan. Indeed you may find, as you try and do this, that the business model and strategy(ies) aren't properly documented either.

Malcolm Whitehouse, IS director and CIO in the UK Government's Department of Work and Pensions (DWP), highlights this process as a critical success factor of any IT–business alignment effort:

> *'You need to bottom out what the operating model for the organisation is and what the end to end processes that run the business are. You can then map the IS/IT capabilities to these end-to-end processes to determine which elements of IT allow the business to do what it does. This provides an understanding of what that means in terms of the different people in different parts of the organisation, what they are doing on a day-to-day basis and what they need to deliver.'*

Angela Yochem, a senior executive at one of the United States' largest banking organizations, suggests such a process:

> *'Technology leaders need to change the way we look at the business functions we support. A great way to start is to ignore organizational boundaries in favor of logical groupings of functions, processes and systems. For each grouping, assess how each business area uses technology. This should include the costs of maintaining redundant systems and skills, identify IT conflicts and overlaps, and a "straw man" prioritisation for optimisation. Once you have that view, you can see if it can be reconciled to your business strategy and the known direction of the industry. The result is a "heat map" showing where you* **should** *be making IT investments (in contrast to where they may have been made historically).*
>
> *This sort of exercise is not easy, nor is it quick, but this sort of analysis is what's required before you can have a meaningful conversation with the business about investment strategy. I've seen this sort of activity require three people full-time for six*

months – but the price tag on such an exercise is far overshadowed by the potential savings.'

Yochem is very clear that this process can advance the state of IT–business alignment in an organisation:

'Think of the effect of having such detailed technology investment profile – existing and proposed – from the IT organisation. The line-of-business champions are forced to justify their own planned investments in this context rather than simply saying "we want to roll out a new system" or the like. Historically those business heads may have driven IT investment unquestioned. This model requires all partners to sit down and work together to figure out what's really necessary – to prioritise their investments appropriately.'

Overcoming the sceptics

In our work with organisations over the years, we've encountered many situations where the recommendations outlined above have met with incredulity. Figure 6.6 below summarises some of the responses often heard from busy business and IT executives.

Addressing these very valid concerns comes down to educating all concerned about the importance and centrality of one thing: *strategy*.

Figure 6.6: The sceptic's questions

Most of the time, these concerns come to the fore when the person's role and responsibilities in the context of the organisation's strategies are unclear. Either the person doesn't understand why, at a fundamental level, IT–business alignment is important, or they don't understand why their particular area has to get involved. In either case, the answers are likely to come from their understanding the organisation's strategy and how that strategy depends on the IT to be delivered that works 'horizontally' across the business to drive operational consistency and integration.

It's going to be a rare organisation indeed that doesn't have this kind of feature as a critical success factor in realising its strategies. We'd argue that any senior IT or business executives raising questions like those in Figure 6.6 above are anachronistic – they need to sign up for training or look for employment elsewhere.

Nick Malik from Microsoft explains the problem that the enterprise architecture team often faces and how the company deals with it:

*'The challenge is invariably about convincing someone that in order to make things better, they have to spend a bit more up front – and that extra spending will end up making **other people's** lives easier. This is because in implementing a new requirement they need to spend some money to harmonise that new requirement with a common "system of record", rather than just building the new functionality from scratch. Doing this is a bit like saying, "you're the first person to want to drive between Kansas and New York, so you're going to need to pay to have all the bridges built on the route." The client says, "no way." How do you persuade them?*

*There are two elements to resolving the issue. The first is to go back to the business strategy of that customer and say, "you know what, you're going to come back to me with another requirement next year for something similar and if we do it this way, then next year you'll pay a lot less. And I know you're going to come back to me next year, because it says here in this strategy document that you're working towards this larger goal." So the first piece is about being savvy about business strategy and using knowledge of that to win your arguments about future investments and the value of architecting longer-term solutions. The second is to work hard to figure out which of the bridges **have** to be built for this one project, and which can be pulled together with baling wire in the short term – which bits of functionality can be brought from other systems for example – to minimise the extra investment. That means that this second piece requires a clear understanding of the whole IT real estate and what it can do.*

The key is to get all the right people to agree, first off, what the core principles are on which decisions should be made. This has to be done but it can take a lot of effort. Enterprise Architecture has quite a lot of clout in Microsoft but still you can't force unpopular decisions through – you have to be able to convince people why it's vital to spend a bit more money up front to get a better result in the long term.'

Darin Brumby, CIO of First Group, puts it more succinctly when talking about how IT strategy has to reflect the business strategy – and therefore why thinking about the strategic value of IT can't just be delegated to the IT department:

'Whenever I've been asked to create an IT strategy in a vacuum, I've said - so why aren't you starting from being brave enough to take your own risks? I'm not crafting you an IS strategy until we spend the next 6 weeks and work out the strategy of the organisation.'

Maintaining alignment

Plan for change

The ITGB process has to be about spotting internal or environmental changes and making adjustments to road maps and strategy documents accordingly. It's worth highlighting what a couple of our interviewees had to say about the importance of planning for change.

Nick Malik, Enterprise architect at Microsoft:

'Partitioning your IT domain and optimising each partition for different things (eg cost, flexibility etc) makes a lot of sense but you have to realise that the drivers within each of those domains will change and so your domain optimisations will have to change too. The domain boundaries might shift as well. So you're dealing with multiple levels of change. The answer? Renew (not just revisit) your IT strategy every year and look again at all the assumptions you've made. Six months is too often – it creates too much thrashing. A review interval of more than a year isn't often enough.'

Our anonymous multinational financial services organisation IT director agrees:

'There is a move to drive consistent technology road maps across the different IT towers. Historically this has not been done.

Now, 3-year road maps are shared with the line-of-business and line-of-business/ application development plans are shared with core IT. This provides shared visibility and the opportunity to attempt to align where the business wants to take things with what the infrastructure team plans to deliver to support them. The road maps are driven by the Engineering Board. There is a group that is responsible for defining templates for the road maps; defining the road map schedule. Road maps are refreshed and submitted every 6 months and deviations from this schedule are reported to the Engineering Board.

The road maps really help in terms of providing visibility, and helping limit surprises and providing shared understanding.'

To deal with change, the ITGB process should ensure that

- The ITGB meets regularly – quarterly is a good interval

- Prior to each meeting, the ITGB should invite business and IT executives to submit proposals for new investments or to justify significant planned changes to existing investments

- At each meeting the ITGB should review existing road map material and agree on changes and updates that need to be made in order to reflect changes in strategy, operational conditions or other opportunities. Proposals for new or significantly changed IT investments should be reviewed and agreed, rejected or 'sent back for rework'. Annually, the ITGB should undertake a thorough review of the business strategy and road map documents as well as the IT strategy and road maps

Where business opportunities or challenges which have significant IT impacts arise urgently, there must be a mechanism for working with the ITGB outside its regular meeting schedule.

Respond to change

In an ideal world the ITGB process would be able to work at the same pace as business and IT change and according to the same priorities. In reality this ideal state is not going to be reached. There will be tactical project demands, both from the business and IT sides, which will not fit into the process outlined above. Even if it is possible for those project teams to convene extraordinary meetings with the ITGB, they may still need to operate without oversight because the project simply has to be done; for example, to respond to an immediate competitive threat or to comply with new or changed regulations.

In these situations it should be possible for such projects to apply for a dispensation. The key here is to ensure that these exceptions are explicit and that dispensation has to be granted by the ITGB. For the reasons outlined above, it would be all too easy for particular functions to perceive, because of their laser focus, that their requirements are just too important to warrant oversight. Their perception may be correct, but the dispensation process ensures that they are able to justify it and that their justification is shared by all the key stakeholders.

The granting of a dispensation is not the end of it, and the project is only temporarily off the hook. A dispensation should only be granted with the commitment of the team to subject the project to the ITGB review process, at some point in the future that is agreed with the ITGB.

Summary

- One of the challenges most commonly cited in research studies and individual executive interviews we've carried out relates to harmonising the agendas of often divergent groups of business practitioners. Increasingly, strategic IT initiatives fall apart because they require buy-in from diverse groups of stakeholders, and getting agreement between these groups on priorities and goals proves impossible.

- As the footprints of IT investments become ever larger and more intertwined with business processes, however, situations where business teams and departments have to work together in certain areas are becoming increasingly important. The pressures of globalisation, transparency and so on mean that business groups have to come together if organisations overall are going to succeed in driving their strategies forward.

- The core ingredient in creating a set of coordinated goals and objectives is a 'single point of truth' for the discussion and agreement of IT-dependent business initiatives and business-dependent IT initiatives. This needs to be both an organisational construct and a well-defined process. We call it the IT Governance Board (though you can call it anything you like – the name isn't that important, but how it is organised and what it does is!)

- In common with our other principles, although both IT and business teams need to move from their comfort zones to make this work, IT has to make the first move if changes are going to take place. Building a 'straw man' prioritised list of key IT changes, which need to take place if the business is to realise its goals, is a great start and something which will pay dividends (both concretely and in terms of 'brownie points').

7

Manage IT as a business-driven portfolio

The old adage 'don't lose sight of the wood for the trees' is sound advice in many business scenarios and is particularly apt when it comes to managing IT investments. It is all too easy to focus on each system or project individually and become obsessed with success or failure at this detailed level. Effective management of IT investments, however, requires a big-picture view that does not just consider the work that is planned or in progress but also fully encompasses past investments.

A business-driven portfolio approach which is designed to ensure a net overall contribution of value to the business from IT spending, in a manner that considers all significant assets and activity, along with the dependencies between them, provides that big-picture view. The end result is a managed portfolio that balances risks, costs and returns associated with IT investments across the business as a whole.

Common areas of misalignment

The word 'solution' is one that pervades IT industry discussions, particularly within the supplier community. The implication is that IT is all about defining a series of problems and then searching for and implementing solutions that address them – or, even worse, defining solutions and then looking for problems to solve them!

While many in IT and the business object to the marketing connotations of such 'solution speak', when you look at the way many IT organisations work, the spirit is actually not that different. Perhaps the words 'requirement' and 'project' are more relevant in this context, but the basic principle of defining work as a series of discrete packages of activity is definitely there.

This is understandable as in practice, the project-driven approach to evolving and investing in IT is necessary in order to keep control and manage activities effectively. Similarly, it helps to think in terms of individual systems from a maintenance and support perspective.

The danger comes, however, when IT management in general gravitates to the level at which everything is considered on a project-by-project or system-by-system basis with no aggregate or higher level view of what's going on and why, or how the overall technology and business environment at this higher level are changing.

Managing IT as a business-driven portfolio is an approach that ensures this bigger picture view is formulated, maintained and then taken into account when considering new investments or managing assets and past investments to ensure that value overall is maximised, with costs and risks kept to a minimum. In essence, it's about making sure you don't lose sight of the wood for the trees.

Before looking at the approach in detail, let's take a look at some of the specific problems it is designed to address.

The tripwire of change

One thing that is easy to forget is that a sensible looking decision taken at one point in time might no longer make sense 6 months down the line. This may be true when considering existing systems or infrastructure, as well as in relation to projects conducted over an extended period.

The fact is that both IT and business are complex, dynamic systems, whose states are nondeterministic, and therefore, infinitely variable. It should therefore be perfectly normal, for example, to expect a project to change or even be scrapped, only 3 months after it was initially specified on occasions between initial specification and the final scheduled delivery date as Richard Steel, CIO at the London Borough of Newham, points out:

> '*Things change, sometimes faster than you would like: it is not uncommon for the goals of a programme to shift considerably before the programme is complete. You have to recognise, and be able to act upon the effect of changing priorities. These may come from the business environment, changing technologies and cultural evolution, each may result in significant, unexpected change.*'

One of the major causes of change is, of course, technology itself. Not very long ago, it was still seen as normal to suggest that small offices would be equipped with wired computer networks, or that special provision would be made for connecting teleworking employees. Today of course, wireless networks in the office are commonplace and many white-collar employees have both wireless and broadband in their homes, which means that it has become much easier for people to work from home or in isolation from the head office, still with full access to technology facilities.

It is not unheard of for the technologies specified in an IT project or program to be superseded halfway through the process, or worse, like the broadband example, the project itself to be overtaken by events. Equally, there could be a project whose usefulness or ability to respond is seriously undermined by new technology developments. Explains an IT director at a major financial institution (who's asked to remain anonymous):

> '*It can take months to get through the approval processes. Once new or changed IT capabilities have been explained to the business and implemented across the organisation, there is a risk of it being obsolete. You can end up chasing your tail.*'

Blind alleys and cliff edges

Equally, however, it is totally normal in practice for the momentum of a project to drive it forward long after everyone already knows that it is doomed. The simple fact is that people don't like change. This is an indisputable element of human psychology, and yet, it is possibly one of the most significant reasons why so much of IT fails to deliver the value that was originally planned for it.

There are plenty of quite high-profile examples of failing or failed projects such as the UK government's National Insurance Recording System (NIRS2) and Nestle SA's global Enterprise Resource Planning (ERP) deployment; the question is that how many of these could have been stopped at a much earlier point, if it wasn't for people insisting on continuing the project, or, if it wasn't for the fact that there were no controls in place at a high enough level to determine whether or not a project should be shelved or significantly modified?

Unanticipated (or undeclared) outcomes

Even if a project is successful, the chances are it will end up costing more than was originally planned. There are a number of potential reasons for this: perhaps the project was just poorly specified at the start, but maybe this was done deliberately, in the knowledge that if the project had been fully specified, the business case would never have been approved.

Alternatively, a successful project may be seized upon and requested to do more than was originally required of it. A given application may need to support a larger number of users for example, or the usefulness of a network link may only become apparent as it is filled with all kinds of data streams that were not initially planned. Infuriating but true, often it is only when a computer system is delivered that the project's sponsor really works out what the business users of the system need.

Reinventing the wheel

Even when successful, IT projects tend to be discrete entities – once the business case is justified, the project rolls on to completion with little regard for what is happening else-where. There are countless examples of projects being duplicated across organisations – Intranet sites, content management systems, user directories, business intelligence and reporting systems to name just a few – either because one part of the organisation doesn't know (or care) what the rest is up to or because it is just easier to reinvent the wheel than to try to coordinate across projects.

Cycles out of sync

Left to its natural evolutionary tendencies, IT would move forward as a series of over-lapping cycles, as applications, different parts of the infrastructure and different technol-ogies, and so on progress from initial adoption through maturity to obsolescence and end of life.

The problem is that business cycles move quite independently of this, as Darin Brumby, CIO at First Group, explains:

'We've got projects happening in areas of maintenance, innovation, growth and productivity and the business is moving through a cycle of those four things. One month we are in maintenance mode – get those costs down; the next month we are in innovation mode – we've got to move here; then we're in productivity mode – let's get processes efficient, and look at business process outsourcing.'

Trying to get a high-cost project approved when an organisation is in the cost cutting phase of its business cycle can be difficult, and taking time out to implement an infrastructure upgrade when the business is driving into a new market and screaming for innovation is equally hard. The difficulty reconciling the two cycles is a common cause of misalignment between IT and business, and when cycles get out of sync, it can be very frustrating for the IT function that can see the need for certain kinds of investment that do not necessarily fit with the way the business is thinking at the time. Says Carson Booth, EMEA IT Director, Starwood Hotels:

> *'We can never really get ahead of the technology S-curve ... it's almost impossible. The financial side is not under our direct control ... I'm constantly defending why we need to invest in technology – I spend about forty percent of my time doing just that.'*

Unthinking adherence to standard ROI models

IT is an investment that should generate some kind of return. But just how seriously do we treat the idea of 'investment'? As we discussed in Chapter 4, ROI estimation tools are certainly preferable to a model that treats IT as an investment in much the same way as a one-armed bandit – we keep feeding the machine, and every now and then it sputters out a bit of a reward. However, such tools are becoming less able to measure IT value.

One of the problems is that the returns within a project are cumulative – they amass over time, so it makes sense to try for early delivery, as shown in Figure 7.1:

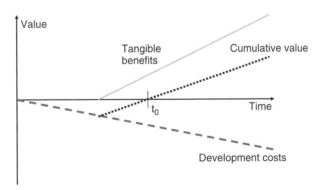

Figure 7.1: Try for early delivery

Such factors are not always taken into account, so while the theory of early returns is clear, the practice is less so, and common sense is all too often usurped by the slavish application of Excel models. As John Johnson, CIO at Intel, points out:

> *'It's very easy to end up with ROI constipation, where the financial returns for each project are scrutinised to the n'th degree, holding up progress through unnecessary delays and the rejection of investments that can add value in other ways.'*

The blinkered view of value

As we discussed in Chapter 6, IT and business are increasingly intertwined, so the usual practice of considering investments in isolation can also be problematic. It is often difficult for future needs, beyond the immediate project, to be accounted for, for example, building a core system in a manner that facilitates integration in the future through a service oriented approach may cost more than building it in a closed manner. In other words, in order to maximise immediate returns, the system is built in a way that is guaranteed to add incremental cost to subsequent projects that must integrate with it. Such false economies are a common product of the piecemeal way in which IT investments are often appraised.

Quietly dripping taps

And while everyone is focussed on managing new investments, it is easy to overlook the fact that the costs associated with some existing systems have been creeping up over time, as patch upon patch has made applications ever more difficult to maintain, technology obsolescence has increased the cost of skills, and so on. It may even be the case that users have gradually drifted away from some systems, as changes in business requirements and processes have made them less and less relevant.

These kinds of changes can happen so gradually that often no one really notices. The IT function just keeps on maintaining and supporting systems unquestioningly, a problem which is exacerbated by the lack of business accountability and ownership which we discussed in Chapter 5. Meanwhile, the cost efficiency, price/performance, flexibility and functionality of newer systems and technologies will have moved on; so if anyone did examine how much money was being spent keeping what's there already up and running, they would probably find resources being squandered on systems that either deliver little value or could deliver the same or more value much more cost-effectively with, for example, a technology refresh.

Alignment imperatives

The overriding imperative is to make sure that the net overall return from IT related spend is significantly positive, but in a way that is realistic and takes into account the way both value and costs accumulate over time via both new and existing systems.

In practical terms, aiming for every project to deliver 100% of the business value that was conceived at the outset is not particularly useful. As Darin Brumby, CIO at First Group, puts it:

> *'In my portfolio I have 220 projects . . . Sure, I'd like Utopian projects which all finish on time and to budget, are highly successful deployments with great post-implementation reviews. In reality I would be happy if just 80% of those just moved along, and were completed. Even if they were just 80% right, I would be happy because the amount of distance that would move this company forward against its competitors in this sector would be enormous.'*

Clearly, there will also be investments that deliver beyond the original expectation, maybe yielding much more value than was planned. As is the way of things, however, it is not generally these over-performing projects that get highlighted when the overall effectiveness of IT investments are reviewed, not least because the way that performance is reported does not reflect the way that the business thinks about value. The tendency is to focus on the failures.

As we have said, the tendency it is also common to regard investments parochially, with little consideration paid to the ongoing cost and contribution equation for the existing systems.

So what's the answer?

Well one approach is to consider IT investment in much the same way as an asset manager in a managed fund would treat investment, by taking into account the portfolio as a whole. A well-designed investment portfolio in the financial world, for example, will blend a series of relatively 'safe' investments to create a baseline that provides for a core of growth and stability, with more aggressive investments which are designed to drive a much higher return but naturally carry higher risks. It will also allow the balance of investments to change in line with changing priorities and objectives, for example, as retirement approaches or children begin to think about university.

The important point, however, is the concept of a portfolio being both balanced and managed. A portfolio completely made up of safe investments will never deliver spectacular returns, and one that contains only high-risk investments stands as much chance of bankrupting its owner as making them rich. From a management perspective, it is then important to constantly reevaluate the components of the portfolio, selling off stocks that are not performing or you suspect will take a performance hit in the future, and keeping an eye open for new opportunities that may be added to maintain strength and balance.

So let's consider how the concept of portfolio management translates into the world of IT, beginning with some guidance for making the necessary adjustments if the approach being used right now is more piecemeal in nature.

Achieving alignment

The way to achieve overall balance between cost, risk and value is to treat the whole of IT as a portfolio, and to manage it accordingly. This means management of the entire IT life cycle from procurement and development through operation and, ultimately, retirement. Within this section, we are not so concerned about management tools such as 'project management' or 'portfolio management' systems. Though there are many of these out there that can help to automate different aspects of the portfolio management process, it is important that there is first a degree of clarity about how an IT portfolio is constructed and maintained in a business-driven manner.

Start with domains and services, not projects

To achieve the power of the portfolio, we need to build the portfolio – potentially from disparate parts of the organisation. We are under absolutely no illusion how difficult this can be. As we have already discussed, just knowing what is out there and how much it is costing is already a significant challenge. Challenging maybe, but this does not make it any less necessary. There are various mechanisms that can be used: clipboard-based audits, automatic discovery tools, reviews of purchase orders and organising of paperwork, all are valid, and it is likely that a combination of approaches will be necessary to arrive at a reasonable view of what is in the IT environment.

The second part of building the portfolio is to group IT assets in some way, so that it is possible to structure the portfolio at a level higher than network cables and computer chips. The goal is to identify a number of 'buckets' or 'domains' which are meaningful to businesspeople and which can drive differentiated IT delivery in line with complex (and sometimes conflicting, in IT terms) sets of business goals and priorities.

As illustrated in Figure 7.2 the concept of managed IT services delivered in the context of business processes provides a logical grouping of IT capabilities that is both recognisable to businesspeople and is a good foundation for identifying discrete domains within the IT landscape.

Note that we have not talked about a project-based grouping of IT investments. While projects offer a useful vehicle for managing the implementation of systems and, therefore,

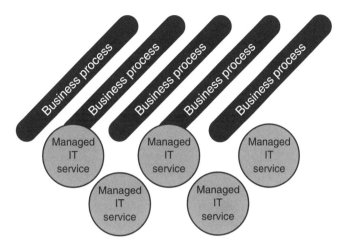

Figure 7.2: A portfolio comprising managed IT services, supporting business processes

the realisation of investments within the portfolio, just as share trades support the implementation of an investment portfolio, we need to get out of the habit of seeing the world only from the perspective of projects. It is the value of what has already been delivered or what is planned to be delivered – which is better explained in terms of services and processes – that should be the focus of the discussion. Effective delivery is important; delivering the right things more so.

Synchronise with business objectives and requirements

Once the portfolio has been defined, it needs to be reviewed against the corporate IT and business strategies we discussed in Chapter 6, as shown in Figure 7.3

Validating the portfolio against business objectives and priorities is really about making sure that the right things are in place, and if not, that appropriate plans exist to fill the gaps and make the necessary adjustments to achieve alignment. This process is also important because it will highlight current and future investments in IT capabilities that do not reflect the needs of the business.

The key is to use the coordinated goals and objectives to partition the portfolio into domains based on business priorities. Within particular domains, the characteristics of the business processes will demand different types of optimisation. For example, business processes which differentiate the business and support management and strategy setting should be optimised for flexibility, whilst those which are a cost of doing business and do not differentiate, should be optimised for efficiency, as shown in Figure 7.4.

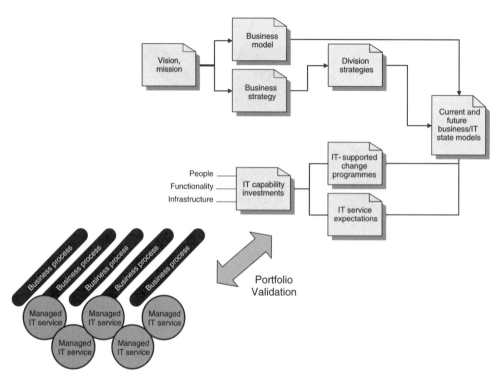

Figure 7.3: Validating the portfolio against corporate IT and business strategies

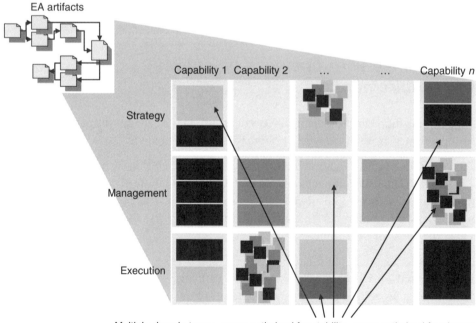

Multiple domain types –some optimised for stability, some optimised for change

Figure 7.4: Domains drive service optimisations, and optimisations drive portfolio management

Requalify work in progress and planned projects…

Once there is an understanding of how well or otherwise existing, ongoing and planned investments map on to business requirements and risks, and the dependencies between them, it is possible to consider the strengths and weaknesses of individual projects objectively, and how they map onto the delivery of business value through the IT Governance Board process we discussed in Chapter 6. In general, projects deliver either new or modified systems, or new or modified infrastructure. In both cases, we can treat this as a unit of delivery, and review them accordingly as part of their acceptance into the portfolio.

Graeme Tozer, Principle Enterprise Architect, TUI, United Kingdom, explains a very pragmatic approach to doing this:

'We have a tiered project review process through which all new IT work projects have to pass. All projects have to work through one questionnaire with us when the project starts up. If the project is greater than £5000 in size there's a further questionnaire; if it's greater than £50,000 there's another. Each questionnaire goes into more detail than the last (however the first is a very basic 8-question form, and if the project is small we let the project team fill it in themselves, and we just check it over). Typically we spend about a week on large projects validating the plans and architectural elements.'

As part of this process, a basic checklist of questions should be used to assess every proposed project, regardless of its size, as part of the IT Governance Board process.

Not all systems and projects are equal, however, so it necessary to differentiate and rationalise aspects of the portfolio, just as any good portfolio manager does. Nick Malik, Enterprise Architect, Microsoft, outlines his approach:

'We've gone through our portfolio using commonality-variability-analysis. This has yielded 16 core system areas (things like manufacturing and customer relationship management), and we're trying to get down to one or two systems for those common areas across the whole company. IT domains were historically organised around chart-of-accounts and this created masses of redundancy.'

Finally, with regard to qualifying and requalifying projects, it is important to consider the dependencies between them. It is often the case that the way in which one project is executed can have an impact on other projects further down the line that are reliant on the output from them. Dealing with this may be as simple as bearing in mind future points of integration between systems and ensuring that software is constructed or implemented in an open enough manner to facilitate this with ease. It may also mean selecting hardware and software platforms and other enabling technologies based on future requirements, and not just those of the immediate project at hand. For example, it's no good building a system on a foundation with limited scalability if a future project is likely to extend that system and increase its usage considerably.

The outcome of this kind of dependency analysis may lead to adjustments in the scope and specification of projects and associated plans.

...*but look beyond projects, too*

The benefit of the portfolio management approach is that it confirms and reconfirms the business context for the delivery of IT capabilities as real services – but this makes no sense if you're only applying the approach to new initiatives. We can't apply portfolio management principles to 'new stuff' only – existing systems in place must be appraised too. Otherwise, we're just perpetuating the current IT process silos that create so many problems.

Identify appropriate investment strategies for each initiative

An approach which works well, once the portfolio framework is in place, is to classify both ongoing service delivery initiatives and new projects according to their 'fit' with what's required to deliver business value within the domain in which they operate, and to use this to identify an appropriate investment strategy for each initiative. There are four basic types as illustrated in Figure 7.5.

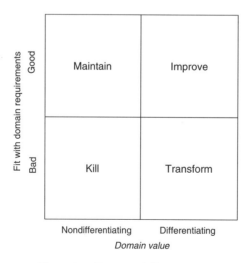

Figure 7.5: Four portfolio strategies

- *Maintain*: this is really a 'business as usual' strategy and should only be applied in situations where a current capability fits the requirements of its portfolio domain well and where the potential return from any changes to the capability is marginal. This is likely to be the case in those domains which correspond to business activities that don't really contribute to overall competitive differentiation. In the real world, where overall budgets are constrained and, therefore, where the 'change bandwidth' has to be allocated intelligently, it makes sense to focus change energy on capabilities where greater returns can be achieved.

- *Improve*: where there is a relatively good fit between a current capability and the requirements of the portfolio domain in which it resides, but where the domain maps to an area of business activity which really does add to competitive differentiation, the best strategy is often to apply a model of continuous, incremental improvement. Nothing's perfect, after all – and if we're looking at an area where IT capabilities really differentiate the business, it's vital that you don't rest on your laurels.

- *Transform*: often in the early stages of introduction of a business-driven portfolio approach, there are significant areas of imbalance where there is a poor fit between the requirements placed on a domain by the governing business activity and some of the IT capabilities within that domain. This is often because systems have previously been built to outdated business requirements or because the technology platform on which a system has been deployed can no longer support the objectives of the business (in the area of integration, commonly). In domains where business activity actively contributes to competitive differentiation, the best strategy to follow is one of transformation. This is not incremental improvement we're talking about, it's radical change.

- *Kill*: one way of looking at the 'kill' strategy is really as the most extreme form of the 'transform' strategy. Where there is a poor fit between an IT capability and the requirements of the domain in which it resides, and where the business activity corresponding to the domain is not the kind of activity that contributes to real competitive differentiation, it often makes most sense to transition away from the existing capability completely.

Clearly the 'kill' and 'transform' strategies bring higher levels of risk than the 'improve' and 'maintain' strategies, assuming that capabilities have been correctly classified (if a capability which really should be 'transformed' is instead classified as 'maintain', this presents a serious risk in itself of course).

In the very common business environment where overall IT budgets are tightly constrained, you have to be smart about how you expose your organisation to risk. The key is to again use your domain analysis to guide the balancing of the strategies that drive out of your portfolio. In domains where competitive differentiation is the core value of business activity and of supporting IT capabilities, you may justifiably shift the balance of strategy towards those that are more risky. In domains where the core value is more about driving efficiency and predictability, it clearly makes sense to err on the side of balancing the portfolio for lower risk levels.

Sort out your budget structures and get control

Nowhere will the level of trust be more important than in the consolidation of the budgets which are to be under the control of the IT organisation. Without such control, it becomes very difficult to make portfolio-oriented investment decisions; however, this doesn't mean the lines of business will give up such control willingly. Explains John Johnson, Intel's CIO:

'At the moment, about a third of spending is outside of central IT budgetary control. There are embedded IT functions in the different divisions and departments that take care of local needs, but a review has shown that this can be wasteful and problematic as local activity is sometimes not very well aligned with the overall strategy, architectural standards, and so on, that are there for good reason. In effect, we are trying to lock down all local IT spending and prevent rogue investments.'

This approach has also been adopted by Thomas Schiller, CIO at Toyota Motorsport:

'I consolidated all of our budgets under IT: now I control all of them, I took them away from the customers so we can make co-ordinated decisions.'

Once control has been gained, it is possible to allocate funding out from the centre, along with other services. This enables a number of benefits:

- Spend can be prioritised more easily in line with strategic business requirements

- The IT function itself can benefit from efficiency savings enabled by merging resources

- Ground rules can be set so that all parts of the organisation use the same criteria with respect to architecture, security, privacy and so on.

Thus, work can take place locally but still with visibility from the centre, maximising efficiency and minimising risk – if it is done right. Of course, if it is ineffective, then work will continue outside of IT. Says John Johnson, CIO at Intel:

'The obvious question is what we do to prevent anarchy and local IT development going underground. In practice, we are not seeing any issues with this as I have people aligned with each business group that are in tune with central IT requirements, so when things get flagged up for approval, they have usually already been through all the checks at local level so there are no surprises.'

Leave adequate room for common sense and instinct

An interesting question that those trying to gain control over IT spend often grapple with, and something we highlighted in Chapter 4, is whether or not it is always necessary to have an explicit financially oriented business case or return on investment model for projects or initiatives. Indeed, it is interesting to consider whether or not anyone trying to make a business case for basic services such as e-mail or even telephony back in the early days would have been able to do so effectively on purely financial grounds. The fact is that there are often investments that may be difficult to cost justify, but where common sense or instinct dictate, they are simply the right things to do.

Darin Brumby, CIO at First Group, cites the example of major airline's installation of self-service ticket machines:

'I spoke with their CIO who said it would never have got off the floor if he had taken the business case for self service ticket machines up through the normal governance process and had to meet the bog standard criteria: NPV hurdle rate at 8%, a return on cash, etc. Even organisations that have progressed their governance to a point where it is possible to get the finances for a new idea, they're still treating too many of them with the traditional finance rules. Some of the great innovations are never going to stack up.'

In such situations, it is essential to focus on the value of the portfolio as a whole rather than on individual IT investments. This allows investments driven by common sense or instinct to be controlled and managed as part of the broader portfolio. Ultimately, that depends on the trust in the portfolio manager – the IT Governance Board–to balance costs and benefits across the portfolio, even where they are unbalanced for individual initiatives. That trust must be earned through a demonstrable ability to manage the portfolio whilst allowing sufficient leeway for innovation. Says John Johnson, CIO at Intel:

'It is really about getting the two working together. If you have a model in place which allows you to deliver value to the business in a positive, measurable and consistent way, you earn the right to go with your instincts on specific initiatives from time to time.'

With this in place, innovation projects can take place without disrupting the mainstream projects and without needing to jump through the same hoops as other projects, as Darin Brumby, CIO at First Group, points out:

'It doesn't necessarily feel like its got to stack up, but experience tells us it will, and we want to be the first to lead in this area, and we want to do a pilot, we want to roll something out, we want to have a go, here it is.'

Maintaining alignment

Once the portfolio is in place, it is important to keep it up-to-date, in particular with the addition of new projects/investments and changing requirements. Portfolio management is about executing on the IT strategy and ensuring that over time, the value of the portfolio increases.

This can be achieved if a few simple principles are borne in mind.

Institutionalise the qualification of new investments

Ensure that a culture of reviewing and qualifying all significant IT investments before funds are committed is instilled into the organisation as we discussed in Chapter 6. At the lowest level, this may be a case of simply completing a page-long questionnaire to ensure that basic checks and balances have been considered and then getting this reviewed by a peer. The level and formality of the review process can be scaled in line with the size and complexity of the investment being qualified, ultimately leading to a structured comprehensive business case being presented at board level for particularly strategic propositions.

Pragmatism is however important. The one thing to be avoided at all costs is process for process' sake. If the objective is to identify and assess even the smallest projects or initiatives, the process for declaring and reviewing them must be simple, otherwise it will not be followed and investments will go underground as previously discussed. An appropriate view of what constitutes a business case is also important. While the purpose and value of every investment should be articulated clearly and precisely, this does not mean that every investment proposal needs a detailed ROI analysis. Having said this, calculating the costs associated with a proposed investment is usually relatively straight-forward, so this element at least should be defined in the majority of cases, says Carson Booth, EMEA IT director at Starwood Hotels:

'Rather than ROI, we're looking at TCO as the lesser of two evils.'

The principle being described here is really no more than making sure the cost and rationale for new investments is always understood, regardless of how that rationale is articulated.

Don't let dead wood accumulate

There comes a point with any investment, when it can no longer generate any further return – when its costs outweigh its benefits, and look like they will for the foreseeable future. In this case, it may well be the moment to turn it off and unplug it, uninstall it or disconnect it from the network.

If the portfolio is being managed effectively, then such systems, projects, services and assets should become apparent, through regular review of the strategy strategic classification you apply to your IT portfolio (as described above). This will not always be the case, though, for example, for systems serving the needs of a particular department – so it is important to undertake periodic tactical investment reviews 'in the field', involving accountable business owners, to determine whether certain investments are approaching that crucial moment. Such reviews should consider a number of questions including:

- How many users are still using the system and how is it changing?

- Are there any other systems or services that deliver similar functionality?

- Are there any new technologies or processes that have led to the system being less usable or relevant than it was?

- Is there anything else preventing the system or service from being accessed?

- What are the operational overheads of using or accessing the system or service?

It is important not to lose sight of the fact that there may be vested interests tied in with investment. For example, a departmental head may not be very happy if a decision is made to put their system 'out to pasture'. For these reasons it becomes even more important to work things out with the business to deal with these 'people effects' says Darin Brumby, CIO at First Group:

> *'It's a case of asking that fundamental question: does this add value? And if it doesn't, why are we doing it? Isn't it a crime when you go into an organisation and you find your top talent working 12, 14, 16 hours a day for you, and you have to go to them and say "You are doing a great job for me, a brilliant job, you are my top performers, but you are working on the wrong thing".'*

Remember why portfolio management is important

Management of a financial portfolio must deal with change, whether it be a slump in the market or a change in priorities. Business agility is about being able to respond effectively to change, and the management of the IT portfolio must facilitate business agility, as Carson Booth, EMEA IT director at Starwood Hotels points out:

> '*We have a number of significant upgrades planned, they're not going to slow down – by the time we're done with one, we're already starting the next. I call this the "pace of innovation". We do try to prepare, try to keep momentum going – it is about being agile.*'

Although adopting a business-driven portfolio management approach will not in itself create the kind of agility necessary, it is an important enabler. Without an objective way of determining the cost, value and risk of proposed activities in the broader context of business priorities, goals and strategies, decision-making remains cumbersome as well as erratic.

Summary

- The problems with managing returns from IT investments are many fold. Failure to recognise or take account of changing requirements during project execution can lead to solutions being delivered in line with the way the business was in the past rather than the way it is today. Excessive emphasis on project level ROI gives rise to short-term false economies and the rejection of investments that lay important infrastructural foundations or deliver significant value, but in ways that are difficult to measure financially. Then we have the problem of lack of visibility and coordination leading to reinvention of the wheel, as various parts of the business invest in similar but different solutions.

- Ensuring an ongoing return from past investments can also be a challenge. All too often, the cost of maintaining existing systems creeps up, while the organisation's dependency on them falls, leading to steady and wasteful drip of IT budget and resources.

- Against this background, it is necessary to form a coherent view of all IT assets and activities and map these onto business priorities, objectives and the services that they support. The cost, value and risk of individual systems and projects may then be reviewed in a business driven context, and decisions made about how best to direct or redirect IT resources on an informed and objective basis, taking both intangible and tangible value into account along the way.

- Once a balanced business-driven portfolio has been constructed in this manner, it must be maintained through institutionalised qualification of all new IT investments and regular reviews of existing investments to prevent dead wood from accumulating. The resources of the IT organisation are then much more likely to remain focussed on what really matters.

8

Foster relationships with key IT suppliers

Supplier relationship management is an important piece of the IT–business alignment jigsaw. Apart from providing IT capabilities, suppliers, if well managed, can represent an invaluable source of skills, resources and insight to help optimise the delivery and support of services to the business. Improper or inadequate supplier management, however, can lead to higher costs, unnecessary risks and failure to maximise return on IT investments.

But developing an effective supplier management strategy and approach is easier said than done, not least because of the range of products and services provided and the various roles played by different suppliers. Here we outline some practical steps that can be taken to first understand who your key IT suppliers are and then to manage your relationships with them objectively, in a win-win manner.

Common areas of misalignment

Effective interaction with and use of suppliers is key to delivering value from IT, not just because they provide many of the IT capabilities required by an organisation but because they can also be a good source of best practice advice, guidance and insight. In addition, their strategies and objectives may have an impact on the organisation's own IT and business strategy, particularly where the supplier is strategic in nature.

When looking at the role of suppliers in IT–business alignment, there are two important factors to consider. First, there are several types of suppliers, including hardware and software vendors, systems integrators, outsource service providers, telecommunication companies and advisors such as management consulting firms and industry analysts. Secondly, not all suppliers are created equal: the amount that you spend and their strategic importance will impact the way that you manage your relationship with them.

But managing suppliers effectively is easier said than done, especially given the wide and varied nature of the products and services they provide, the fact that some of them perform multiple roles and functions, and that on so many occasions, it is necessary to engage more than one supplier simultaneously on the same project or initiative. Mark McAllister, IT director at Giant Group, highlights the challenges:

'Communicating your aims and objectives effectively to the suppliers that you choose to work with in the technology sector, pressing them to deliver what you need as a business imperative from technology, in a manner which isn't always textbook, has been our biggest problem.'

Fragmentation of supplier activity and relationships

In an organisation of any size, there is an ever-present need to procure a wide range of IT products and services to satisfy the demands from many parts of the business. In extreme situations where there is little management of the procurement process, this can lead to a fragmentation issue, with different groups within the IT organisation, even multiple departments across the business, buying the same or similar offerings from different suppliers at different prices and with different terms and conditions.

Fortunately, the majority of organisations do not operate in such complete chaos, but our research shows that fragmentation of procurement and supplier relationships is still, nevertheless, often a problem. It is not uncommon, for example, for the same supplier to be dealing separately with different parts of the business, undermining opportunities for volume discounts and creating additional administrative overhead. It is worse still if

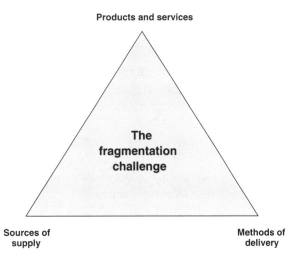

Figure 8.1: Fragmentation complicates the management of supplier relationships

equivalent but different products and services are being bought in a disjointed manner from different suppliers, as this also complicates support and maintenance. Still more fragmentation can arise from the existence of different models for provision of IT capabilities: for example, software-as-a-service versus installed applications; or systems integrator versus offshore development. This adds another dimension to an already complex situation, as shown in Figure 8.1.

One of the consequences of fragmentation is that it can stand in the way of understanding which suppliers are important and why. Without this understanding, there is no objective way to determine which relationships need to be proactively managed, and indeed how. This includes what should be asked of or expected from particular suppliers and how much freedom and influence those suppliers should have in their dealings with the organisation. The absence of proactive relationship management will in many cases open the door for suppliers to assume more control than is in the best interests of the business. As Malcolm Whitehouse, IS director and CIO in the UK Government's Department of Work and Pensions (DWP), puts it:

> *'There is a risk that suppliers do not talk to the organisation with one voice and instead seek to divide and conquer.'*

Allowing the tail to wag the dog

This tendency to divide and conquer is compounded by a characteristic that is common to all suppliers: that their own agenda takes precedence over that of their customers. Of course that's not to say that the latter isn't taken into account; unless customers believe that suppliers are delivering products and services that meet their needs, they would clearly not buy from them. It is more a question of whose agenda comes first, and by default, the suppliers will try to further their own to encourage the procurement of new products, upgrades, among others that allow them to meet their sales targets and other business objectives. As Richard Steel, CIO at the London Borough of Newham, points out:

> 'We find it hard to get IT suppliers to stop selling whatever products are new and start listening to our broader and longer term requirements.'

Beyond this, even if the suppliers have learned to listen, they are still unlikely to recommend or encourage something that is in their customer's interests but not their own. This may sound mercenary, but it is, in fact, just good business practice on the part of the supplier, and there is no reason to expect them to behave any differently.

This is important because suppliers tend to know much more about the specific ideas, technologies and techniques in their chosen domain than the customer as they are living and breathing that domain every day. As a result, they are often in a strong position to influence the customer's view of what's important and what's not. IT sales people are, in fact, trained to guide the customer towards emphasising requirements that play to the strengths and unique selling points of the supplier offering, whilst downplaying those that highlight weaknesses or limitations. If the customer is not careful, this can lead to situations in which the capabilities of the technology solution or service effectively end up as the basis for redefining the business requirement.

When this occurs, the IT organisation can easily be distracted by the supplier proposition, thereby forcing it out of alignment with the needs of the business. This then leads to one of the most common complaints we hear about IT organisations in general: that they are perceived by the business to be working to their own agenda rather than delivering what the organisation really needs.

Fads, fashion and vested interests

Similar misalignment can arise if large industry analyst firms and IT consulting providers are allowed to set the agenda. At any particular moment these kinds of advisory suppliers tend to be promoting a range of the latest technologies and ideas, often creating the impression that their adoption is an imperative for businesses to maintain their competitive edge, operational efficiency and so on; there is always, of course, a sense of urgency in their messages and advice.

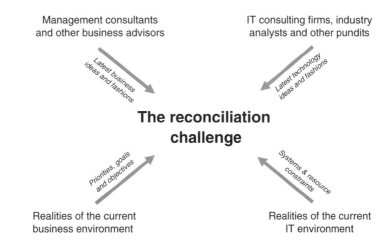

Figure 8.2: **Promotion of the latest technology and business ideas leads to confusion**

As part of this process, such players often invent new terminology, acronyms, categories of solution and so forth. Sometimes this can be useful to further understanding of genuinely new ideas and concepts, but it is often as much about creating opportunities to sell research products or consulting engagements. In other words, by driving a new set of imperatives and new types of offerings, they are looking to generate demand for their own products and services.

And the same thing is occurring on the business side. Management consultants and other business advisors are constantly promoting the latest business ideas to senior management.

The upshot of this, as shown in Figure 8.2, is the need to reconcile the realities of the current business and IT environments with the promotion of the latest technology and business trends and ideas.

It would be great if all of this advice dovetailed together nicely, but often it doesn't. In the 1990s, for example, Enterprise Resource Planning (ERP) with its prescriptive processes was never a particularly comfortable bedfellow of Business Process Reengineering (BPR) which advocated a more 'clean sheet' style of thinking. Today, we have similarly conflicting pulls, at least on the surface, between corporate governance ideas coming out of the business camp and the Web 2.0 concepts promoted by the IT industry.

Whatever the drivers and motivations, the activities and advice of consultants and analysts, while articulated as high-level aspirational and inspirational visions, often lure IT professionals away from the job at hand, that is, ensuring that the business benefits from IT-related investments and activities in a reasonable timescale. Chasing fads, fashions, dreams and visions, while users are complaining about e-mail system performance and the availability and quality of the help desk services is the best way to lose the trust of those in the business, as we discussed in Chapter 3.

Lack of trust

Unfortunately, the cumulative effect of the above challenges over the years has been a strong tendency to mistrust IT suppliers, who are often perceived to have taken advantage of their customers, whilst not always delivering against promises and expectations.

Whether deserved or not, such mistrust stands in the way of developing and maintaining the most effective kind of win-win relationships which can, in some extreme cases, degenerate to the point where they are adversarial in nature. At that point everyone starts focusing on legal terms in contracts and getting the better of the other party in negotiations. Along the way, a win-lose mentality develops, which invariably leads to a lose-lose outcome, and the value of positive and proactive relationships is lost.

This is a shame because with the right relationship in place, suppliers are often extremely forthcoming with knowledge and insights, effectively free advice, which customers can only benefit from. There is also a potential exposure here as allowing an unhealthy relationship to persist with a supplier whose support and cooperation is critical to the business means that the supplier is much more likely to exploit their leverage at times when the organisation most needs them. When it comes to supplier relationships, legal terms and penalty clauses are no substitute for a spirit of mutual respect and cooperation.

Alignment imperatives

At the highest level, the supplier relationship imperative is summed up by Darin Brumby, CIO at First Group:

'There are three key relationships – my service suppliers, my technology suppliers and my business clients. Communicating our aims and objectives effectively to the suppliers we have chosen to work with in the technology sector, and getting them to deliver that which we need to look after our business clients, has been one of our biggest problems.'

Malcolm Whitehouse, IS director and CIO in the UK Government's Department of Work and Pensions (DWP), expresses a similar view:

'We use multiple suppliers for different capabilities and it is important that we define a clear set of responsibilities and accountabilities which the suppliers are prepared to sign-up for.'

The clear message here is that supplier management is part of the overall equation and that activities in this area must be aligned with the needs of the business. Unless these needs are well understood, it is very difficult to manage supplier relationships objectively.

This means that the principles we discussed in Chapter 6 must be established and applied, at least at a high level, in order to provide the business context required to determine how best to deal with the suppliers.

The other main input into the process of supplier relationship optimisation is the business-driven IT portfolio we discussed in Chapter 7. This provides a prioritised view of the IT capabilities required to meet business goals and objectives which is necessary to highlight supplier dependencies, as shown in Figure 8.3.

Given the challenges outlined above, there are a number of steps which must be followed to foster the effective relationships with key IT suppliers which are so important for IT–business alignment:

- Identify the key suppliers that are particularly important to the organisation achieving its goals and objectives, with reference to the business-driven IT portfolio

- Determine what the organisation needs and wants from each of these key suppliers on a case-by-case basis. This will not only include elements dictated by key IT initiatives

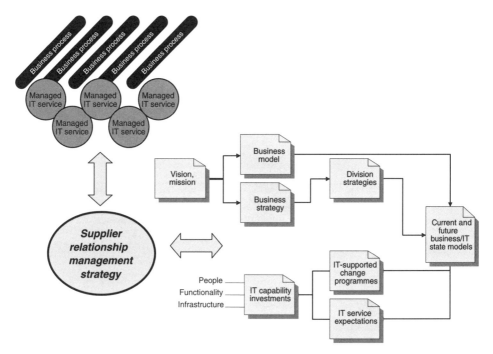

Figure 8.3: Supplier relationships must be managed in line with business and IT objectives and the IT capabilities which underpin them

reflected in the IT portfolio but also address more strategic aspects in line with business and IT goals and objectives

- Establish what these key suppliers need and want from the organisation in return – not simply in terms of the revenue they are looking to generate from the relationship, but also in terms of the potential contribution the organisation can make in other ways, such as helping the suppliers to develop their own business and offerings

- Develop a win-win engagement approach which delivers mutual benefit as defined above

- Develop a process through which non-key suppliers are managed effectively, in the most coordinated and cost-effective manner possible

Achieving alignment

Analyse the supplier base

In order to identify key suppliers, it is first necessary to define what a key supplier actually is. At one level, it is possible to identify key suppliers through some kind of subjective judgement, but it is far more useful to work through a more precise set of criteria.

To begin with, suppliers may be broadly grouped in accordance with the level of spend and level of criticality to the business. This gives rise to an initial categorisation as shown in Figure 8.4.

Grouping suppliers in this way is a good starting point, since it is possible to immediately put aside all noncritical, low-volume suppliers from a proactive relationship management

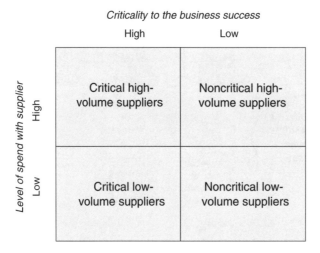

Figure 8.4: Categorise suppliers in terms of spend and business criticality

perspective. If the spend is low and what's being provided is essentially commodity or utility in nature, then it is perfectly adequate to deal with the supplier on a transaction-by-transaction basis through an efficient procurement process.

It is also fairly straightforward figuring out the high-level objectives for managing noncritical high-volume suppliers. This could, for example, be a supplier from which the organisation routinely buys PCs, commodity servers, standards-based networking equipment, telecom services and so on. Although the organisation is likely to be reliant on such suppliers to deliver and support their solution(s) and/or services to maintain service levels to the business and manage costs effectively, a switch to another supplier, if necessary or desirable, could be made without incurring significant incremental cost, risk or disruption to the business.

This leaves critical suppliers as a broad group to meet the following criteria:

- The organisation is dependent on the supplier's solution(s) and/or services to remain operational and effective

- Switching to an alternative supplier would incur significant expense, disruption and/or risk to the business

- The supplier's plans or direction for its solution(s) and/or services have a tangible impact on the organisation's own plans

When it comes to these suppliers, that is, those whose solutions or services are deeply embedded into the organisation's IT infrastructure and operational landscape, it is important to distinguish them further according to another criterion – the level of strategic alignment.

Regardless of their size and the level of spend, any supplier whose solution(s) or services are considered to be important strategically and whose own objectives, direction and plans are in tune with those of the organisation, should be classified as strategic.

In practice, the likelihood is that most organisations will have a relatively small number of genuinely strategic suppliers, the candidates being core business application vendors (e.g. ERP or supply chain management systems), software infrastructure vendors (e.g. core middleware and database platforms) and critical service providers (e.g. outsourcing, systems integration and possibly telecoms). It is also important to recognise that in some instances, a supplier may be strategic in some areas and not in others, but when this happens, it is still wise to manage the relationship as a whole on a strategic basis.

Finally, there are critical suppliers that are not strategically aligned, with the most common examples being the suppliers of legacy capabilities or capabilities based on technologies, techniques or standards that are in conflict with the organisation's chosen direction. In such cases, it is most appropriate to reduce the organisation's dependency on those capabilities over time, or at least to contain it. Either way, the relationship must be proactively managed. If it isn't, then there is the distinct possibility that a strategic conflict will arise unexpectedly in the future: for example a critical system that has been 'frozen' because it no longer aligns with the strategic direction of the organisation, but the version being used has been 'end-of-lifed' by the supplier. This then forces a choice to either invest in an upgrade to a subsequent release that does not fit with the overall strategy or migrate under pressure to a strategically aligned alternative and incur an element of unplanned and unwanted risk.

Establish high-level objectives

In order to define specific requirements for the management of your key suppliers, it is first necessary to define high-level objectives for the different types of suppliers discussed above. Figure 8.5 provides a representative frame of reference, which should be optimised for the particular needs of your organisation.

With such a frame of reference in place, it is then possible to focus on the suppliers which are important because they are critical and/or the level of spend with them is high: the first three groups in Figure 8.5.

Type of supplier	Characteristics	Objectives
Strategically aligned critical (high and low volume) suppliers	The organisation is dependent on the supplier's offerings to remain operational and effective, and to achieve its longer term goals and objectives, and the supplier's strategy is aligned with that of the organisation.	Manage the relationship on a proactive basis with an effective and relevant two-way dialogue and a mutually beneficial win-win engagement plan.
Strategically misaligned critical (high and low volume) suppliers	The organisation has a similar level of short-and long-term dependency as outlined above,but the supplier's direction and strategy are not a good fit with those of the organisation.	Manage the relationship proactively but with a focus on containment and/or reduction of dependency and risk over time.
Noncritical high-volume suppliers	Suppliers of commodity or utility solutions/services that are not strategic in nature, but represent a significant level of spend and must be adequately supported for the organisation to remain operational and effective.	Manage the relationship proactively with a focus on commercial and operational efficiency. The objective here is to optimise the cost/value equation and ensure adequate support while the supplier is in place.
Noncritical low-volume suppliers	Suppliers of commodity or utility solutions/services, but with whom the organisation has a relatively low level of ongoing spend.	Manage interaction on a transaction-by-transaction basis, in line with an efficient and effective procurement model.

Figure 8.5: An example of supplier management objectives for different types of suppliers

Define requirements and objectives for key suppliers

Unless there is a clear understanding of what is required from a key supplier, it is impossible to assess and track the changes in the effectiveness of the relationship and the performance of that supplier in general.

Many requirements are likely to be common to all key suppliers, such as

- A suitably qualified, experienced and motivated day-to-day accounts or relationship manager, preferably one that doesn't change at the beginning of each new financial year

- Insight into how the supplier works, ranging from the allocation and availability of resources via the account management route, through the way that sales quotas and financial accounting periods work, to sign-off mechanisms for special commercial terms and discounts

- A clear and favourable commercial relationship that allows the relevant solution(s) and/or services to be procured at a good price, on suitable terms and in a predictable manner

- An unambiguous agreement, based on well-defined service levels (if appropriate) to ensure that the supplier is committed to responding in an effective and timely manner in areas such as delivery, support, maintenance and so on

- Commitments to support and maintain older systems and releases of solutions (as appropriate) for a reasonable period of time and at reasonable cost

- Agreed lines of communication to enhance efficiency and prevent fragmented or uncoordinated activity

- An executive level contact with the authority to make things happen if normal processes and procedures fail to satisfy expectations

These requirements are equally applicable to strategically misaligned suppliers, for risk management and mitigation purposes.

Homing in on strategic suppliers, the following requirements should also be considered to ensure the ongoing alignment of goals and objectives:

- An executive level sponsor who maintains a knowledge of the customer organisation and peer level relationships with its senior management based on an open and constructive dialogue

- A mechanism to ensure that the organisation maintains an ongoing knowledge of the supplier's strategy, plans and road maps for future solution and/or service development

- A mechanism for the supplier to take on board the organisation's wishes and requirements and consider them for inclusion in product plans, road maps and so on

- Strategic level advice and guidance on how to get the most from the supplier's solution(s) and/or services as both the business and the supplier offerings evolve

- A willingness and mechanisms in place to work with other suppliers that have a need to integrate or interact with the strategic solution(s) and/or services being provided

As already mentioned, these requirements provide a generic checklist of things to consider. It is important that these are translated to more specific requirements for each supplier on a case-by-case basis. It may, for example, be more important to be kept up-to-date on certain aspects of the supplier's strategy and plans that are particularly relevant to your organisation. Similarly, it may be necessary for a particular supplier to work with another supplier.

The general rule here is that the more specific the organisation can be in terms of its requirements from a supplier relationship, the more likely it is to be able to secure them.

In practical terms, when formulating the 'wish list' of requirements for a particular key supplier, it is essential to gather as much relevant information and input as possible. A good starting point is the IT portfolio we discussed in Chapter 7 to derive supplier dependencies and requirements and prioritise them in line with the importance, contribution, risks and costs associated with key IT initiatives.

It is also important to speak with representatives from across the organisation, from not only the departments impacted by the supplier's solution(s) and/or services but also the legal and accounting departments, who can provide a financial and contractual perspective on the relationship. Developers and operations and support personnel are also a valuable source of insights regarding how well the supplier's offerings are meeting the requirements for utility, functionality, stability, performance and so on at a technology level.

This may seem like a lot of time and effort, but if the organisation is spending 6, 7 or sometimes 8 figure sums on a supplier or is dependent on the supplier to meet its strategic and operational objectives, a comparatively small upfront investment to get the relationship onto the appropriate footing is highly worthwhile. Without it, the supplier will assume more control in the relationship, which can lead to an imbalance.

On this note, it is important to preempt supplier activities and actions wherever possible by improving your knowledge of the supplier and anticipating or agreeing to their requirements.

Get to know your key suppliers

It could be argued that suppliers' needs are irrelevant, provided they commit to deliver what the organisation wants in the way that it wants it. Such a view, however, is very short-sighted. If the organisation can help the supplier to achieve its goals and objectives, then the supplier is much more likely to reciprocate in both tangible and intangible ways. This is the essence of the win-win relationship, which will be by far the most valuable and profitable for both parties in the long run.

Key suppliers will all share a common set of requirements of their customers, including:

- A clear description of the organisation's hierarchy and associated management structure

- Access to relevant personnel, including executives, other key decision makers and/or influencers, enterprise architects and so on

- An understanding of the organisation's business and IT strategy at an appropriate level of detail to support an effective relationship

- Insights into the way the organisation works from a management- and decision-making perspective, such as investment evaluation and sign-off processes, policies for budgeted versus discretionary spend and so on

- Future procurement plans relevant to the supplier, including allocated budget, key decisions over the coming year

- Participation in the supplier's reference programme, for example by agreeing to speak about success stories with other customers and prospects, the media and so on.

In addition, key suppliers will often be looking for detailed insight into specific plans and activities relating to how their solution(s) and/or services are being used and how this is likely to change. Closely related to this, they will often appreciate the customer's participation in improvement programmes, whether on a one-to-one basis or via 'customer councils' and the like.

The extent to which an organisation chooses to meet these requirements depends on the nature of the objectives of the relationship with that supplier. Similarly, the relative importance of these requirements to particular suppliers will vary, and so it is important to find out as much as you can about suppliers' objectives in order to develop an effective engagement plan. That plan also depends on an understanding of the supplier's organisational structure, decision-making processes, financial performance, longer term objectives and so forth.

Develop a win-win engagement plan

Armed with a clear understanding of the different types of suppliers you have, a framework of objectives for the management of key suppliers and an appreciation of how they operate and their requirements, the definition of an engagement plan for each key supplier is relatively straightforward. The preliminary dialogue to understand the supplier's requirements should have identified the appropriate contacts at an executive, sales and operational level. If not, the relevant introductions need to be made and people need to start talking to each other.

The important first step to creating an effective and proactive win-win relationship is to ensure that there is mutual understanding at an executive level. It is necessary to identify executive sponsors on both sides of the relationship and to ensure that they develop a mutual understanding of each other's plans and requirements at a strategic level. From here, objectives should be set for the relationship itself, which may manifest themselves in the form of synchronised spending and delivery plans, alignment of expectations and commitments with regard to performance or service levels, agreement to work jointly towards achieving particular goals such as the implementation of a new capability and so on. It is difficult to generalise here, but it is important to flush out what is pertinent to each party and to agree how each of the elements will be dealt with within the framework of the relationship.

As part of this strategic alignment process, it is important that the parties show an equal commitment. At one level, this might translate into the exchange of confidential information under nondisclosure or the mutual allocation of the resources required to support a particular goal or initiative. While still relatively rare, it may even involve performance-based remuneration of the supplier, which is the ultimate in terms of mutual 'skin in the game'.

This strategic alignment activity should be followed with some of the more detailed requirements outlined previously. Typically, there is a focal point for this kind of discussion on the supplier side in the form of the account manager, and it helps a great deal if the customer reciprocates by ensuring that a relationship manager is identified on its side to act as a counterpart. The 'service manager' we discussed in Chapter 5 is ideally suited to fulfil this role. In practice, however, there will be many other people involved in the interactions between the two organisations, as well as the account manager and relationship manager responsible for the coordination. Having said this, the importance of focal points for relationship management, backed up with appropriate deputies and an escalation process, should not be underestimated.

It is also very useful for the plan to be properly documented. In some cases, this may translate to detailed planning documents, and in others it may be in the form of a simple presentation that captures the aspects.

Determine how to deal with non-key suppliers

The biggest risk with non-key suppliers is fragmentation and the resulting inefficiencies in financial, support and maintenance terms. It is beyond the scope of this book to go into detail on routine procurement best practice, but it will suffice to say that organisations need a process which ensures that money is not wasted by going to the wrong suppliers for the wrong things and that unnecessary risks and overheads are not created through the uncontrolled introduction of capabilities that do not fit.

The process for dealing with non-key suppliers should consider the following:

- Organisation standards, including technology specifications, price expectations (e.g. acceptable level for a notebook PC of a particular class), minimum terms and conditions with regard to payment terms, support and maintenance

- Clear sign-off procedures, with IT endorsement of particular types of purchase to ensure that they are consistent with the overall IT systems architecture, including interoperability standards, support and maintenance model, security requirements and data reliability requirements

- Provisioning requirements, to ensure that equipment and other solutions are properly deployed and accounted for through the use of asset registers or Configuration Management Database (CMDB) updates, preparation by IT (to ensure security, monitoring, backup, etc) and relevant training

With more and more equipment and services being procured independently of the central IT organisation, such as mobile devices, commodity PC equipment, personal productivity software and so on, it is important that the procurement process embraces the necessary elements to ensure that solutions which are not aligned with IT or business requirements are, wherever possible, prevented from entering the organisation.

Maintaining Alignment

Continuously monitor and drive performance

Putting a plan into place as the foundation for managing supplier relationships is only the start. From that point onwards it is necessary to review progress against the plan on a regular basis, both internally and in collaboration with the supplier. It is also, of course, necessary to update the plan in line with changing events and requirements on either side of the equation.

The relationship manager will generally be responsible for making this happen, in collaboration with service managers, project managers and others who are either interacting with the supplier directly or whose activities are dependent on its performance. In some cases, it may even be appropriate to remunerate the relationship manager and other key people involved with the supplier for achievement in line with the objectives of the engagement plan, whether this is measured on an ongoing basis or through the achievement of specific goals.

On a periodic basis, as each business evolves, it is necessary to review the relationship at a strategic/executive level and, where necessary, reset overall priorities, objectives, expectations and commitments. The frequency with which this takes place is clearly dependent on circumstances and may be very high in times of significant change and lower at others.

Keep the dialogue going

Beyond formal relationship management, by far the most the most effective way of ensuring a healthy ongoing relationship with key suppliers is just to keep the dialogue going. Whether this is through the formation of virtual teams, regular review meetings or other techniques, the more people talk across the customer-supplier divide, the more likely a productive and harmonious relationship will prevail.

Advances in collaboration technology can really help here. As we discussed in Chapter 4, real time communication, ideally face to face, over the phone or via instant messaging is preferable to e-mail, which can sometimes create as many problems as it solves – a misinterpreted turn of phrase can so easily lead to offence being taken which then escalates to a full-blown conflict over the course of a few exchanges.

As John Johnson, CIO at Intel, puts it:

> *'Most conflict situations in IT can be avoided if people just talk to each other.'*

Summary

- Poor or inadequate supplier management can lead to fragmentation of the way in which products and services are procured, which in turn results in higher overall costs, increased support overheads and failure to fully unlock the potential value of IT investments. It can also endow individual suppliers with too much power to drive their own agendas, which may not always be aligned with those of the business.

- In order to optimise the way in which suppliers are managed, it is first necessary to identify which suppliers are important and why. Analysing suppliers according to the level of spend with them, the criticality of their solutions or services to the business, and the degree to which their strategy and direction are aligned with those of the organisation provides a framework within which relationship management activity may be prioritised on an objective basis.

- This kind of analysis typically leads to three categories of suppliers that must be proactively managed: critical suppliers who are strategically aligned with the business;

critical suppliers who are strategically misaligned with the business; and noncritical suppliers for whom the organisation's spend is significantly high.

- Effective relationships must be developed with all such suppliers based not just on the goals and objectives of the business but also on those of the supplier. This requires a good understanding of each key supplier beyond the solutions and services that are immediately on offer, and executive level as well as operational level communication and involvement from both parties.

- Once effective relationships are in place, they must be maintained to ensure ongoing alignment via performance reviews and continuous dialogue, with the objectives of keeping communication flowing as freely as possible and ensuring activity is properly coordinated in line with business requirements.

9

Applying the principles

With an understanding of our six principles in place, the important question is how can you apply them? In this chapter we bring all the advice and insights presented in our six principles together by detailing a series of four goals, each of which improves alignment in a precise way by drawing on aspects of each principle.

Following that, we dive a little more into the detail of Enterprise Architecture, which is a capability that underpins many aspects of our alignment principles – showing how it contributes towards the overall alignment agenda and highlighting the importance of a pragmatic, business-driven approach.

Lastly, we introduce and explain the concept of 'agile alignment', an approach to pursuing an IT–business alignment agenda that will help you maximise the sustainability of your efforts by working incrementally and managing for continual change.

Four goals for sustainable IT–business alignment

If you've got this far through the book and have read our six principles for sustainable IT–business alignment, it's probably become obvious that the principles themselves don't immediately suggest a natural ordering of work or road map. Indeed, the number of cross-references between the 'principles' chapters should illustrate that the reality is that all of the principles are intertwined.

So, is there any kind of order of work that makes sense? Luckily, the answer is 'yes'. Our research has shown that there is a straightforward chain of four goals that build on each other, where the principles can be applied in various ways to transform the alignment of IT with business in a stepwise fashion. At the beginning of this book we described the relationship between an IT organisation and its customers as being like two people locked in a small box; the chain of goals we present here enables business and IT to coordinate their actions so that neither gets an eye gouged or a foot stuck in an awkward place.

As Figure 9.1 shows, the chain of goals is as follows:

1. *Gain trust from the business* through being seen as a trusted provider of IT services that 'just work'

2. *Understand and reflect the business* through offering business support from IT services that is differentiated based on the nature of business activity being supported

3. *Engage the business* through roles and activities that tie the IT organisation and the wider business together both in day-to-day delivery of services and in setting IT and business strategy

4. *Drive the business* through business innovation based on understanding of IT and business capabilities and constraints and how they relate to one another

It's important to realise that this chain of goals has to be considered in the context of the needs of the business. It may not always make sense for IT to 'drive the business', for example, in an area of the business which has no desire or need to be driven by IT.

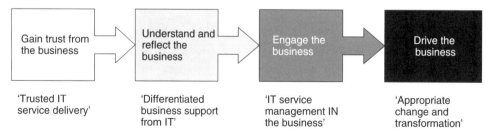

Figure 9.1: A chain of four goals for sustainable IT-business alignment

However, our contention is that although there will be areas where the scope of IT's transformational role has to be constrained, in *every* organisation there will equally be business activities where it does make sense to attempt to achieve all four of the goals above. The trick is to tune your approach according to which part of the business you're thinking about and adjust your efforts accordingly. We tackle this topic in more detail in the section *Agile alignment*.

The goals build on each other

Although our six core principles for sustainable IT–business alignment are intertwined and there's little obvious path through them as isolated ideas, this higher level chain of goals, where groups of principles are applied together, is difficult to traverse in any order other than that shown in Figure 9.1.

This is crucial to understand as you start out on your journey because our research has shown that the majority of CIOs believe that although they're hampered in their work by a lack of trust from the business and a crippling degree of distraction focused on day-to-day firefighting, the most effective route to achieving sustainable IT–business alignment is to have the CIO in a role at the top of the organisation, reporting to the CEO.

This is a seductive thought – that if only the boss of IT was at the top of the organisation as a whole, everything else could be fixed. But it's not practical. Those CIOs who have succeeded in making themselves key drivers of their businesses and whom we have spoken to have made it clear that you can only get into this position if you've started by earning the trust of the business, if you've been proactive in taking steps to remake IT so that it reflects the business' goals and priorities and if you've taken appropriate steps to engage the business in the work of the IT organisation. In short, a top spot for the CIO is an outcome of better IT–business alignment – it's not one of the initial enablers.

With this in mind, then, how do you go about tackling these goals, and how do the different alignment principles we've highlighted contribute to each goal?

Goals and principles

By way of an overview, Figure 9.2 shows each goal, together with the principles which you should apply to help you reach it. In the following sections we expand on each goal and look at the application of the principles in a little more detail.

Goal 1: gain the trust of the business

As we've said a great many times throughout this book, we've come to the conclusion through our research that a lack of trust in IT – and in IT organisations – is a major barrier

	Gain the trust of the business	Understand and reflect the business	Engage the business	Drive the business
The IT organisation must get the basics right	✳✳✳	✳	✳	✳
Create a common language	✳✳	✳✳✳	✳✳✳	✳✳✳
Foster relationships with key IT suppliers	✳	✳✳✳	✳✳✳	✳✳
Manage IT as a business-driven portfolio	✳	✳✳✳	✳✳	✳✳✳
Work towards shared goals and objectives	✳	✳✳✳	✳✳✳	✳✳✳
Establish a peer relationship between business and IT	✳	✳✳	✳✳✳	✳✳✳

Key: ✳✳✳ Highly important   ✳✳ Somewhat important   ✳ Less important

Figure 9.2: The contribution of principles to our alignment goals

to improved IT–business alignment. Creating trust is the first goal you need to achieve because without trust in IT within the business, you will find it very difficult indeed to achieve the other goals.

Creating that trust is primarily a matter of 'getting the basics right'; however, aspects of the 'create a common language' principle are also important, as reflected in Figure 9.2.

'Getting the basics right' is all about transforming the core capabilities of the IT organisation in two ways:

- Layering a 'service management' capability on top of the existing technology management capabilities that are likely to dominate your current organisation;

- Implementing repeatable and managed processes to formalise and improve the quality of the IT activities that are responsible for procuring, creating, deploying, operating and changing IT services throughout their life cycle.

Service management: customer-friendly supply management

From the perspective of our high-level alignment goals, the purpose of IT service management is to create an IT supply management capability that is framed in a way that naturally makes sense to the ultimate consumers of that supply – the organisation's employees, customers, partners and suppliers. We're not advocating service management just because it's elegant! We're doing it because it's a way to cleanly separate what IT cares about (how everything works), from what everyone else cares about (whether it's working or not, and – sometimes – how much it's costing).

Implementing a true service management capability is not something you can simply layer on an existing technology-focused organisation, however. You have to change working practices in order to break down the operational practice silos that commonly constrain and separate development projects and maintenance programmes, and which isolate expertise in the administration of different kinds of technology (databases, operating systems, network elements, middleware, application suites, etc.).

Connecting interface and implementation

In this context, the value of implementing repeatable processes for key IT operation and management activities is about more than improving the outcomes of individual activities (reducing errors introduced by changing a software component, for example) – it's also about forcing the IT organisation to realign itself around service delivery rather than project and operational technology management. You still need technology management capabilities, of course – the need for that hasn't gone away. But for a service management approach to be successful, you have to put organisational linkages in place that span service, project and operational technology management disciplines. If service management is the interface between the IT organisation and the 'customer', project and operational technology management disciplines provide the implementation of that interface. The interface and the implementation must be properly connected.

Feeding back in business terms

Beyond 'getting the basics right', it's vital that your move to implement service management discipline is coupled with changing the ways in which the IT organisation provides feedback – as we discussed in Chapter 4. All your work on creating business-meaningful service interfaces into IT capabilities will come to naught if you can't effectively communicate how you're doing to the IT organisation's 'customers'. This is about more than providing coarse-grained, aggregated feedback: more fundamentally, this is about measuring and reporting on metrics that themselves make sense to those 'customers'.

By way of an example, it's not enough to shift from providing feedback on the transaction processing performance of individual servers supporting an e-commerce system, to providing feedback on the round-trip response time of a transaction from the customer's browser to a back-end system: in that transition you might be changing the granularity of the feedback, but you're still measuring and reporting on something that in itself is unlikely to be interesting to the business owner of the organisation's e-commerce channel. It's far more valuable, say to provide feedback on the number of customers who report unsatisfactory performance – perhaps through inviting customers to take part in satisfaction surveys once they've completed transactions using the system.

If you're in a situation where you have these organisational capabilities in place, you can move to the second goal: understanding and reflecting the business.

Goal 2: understand and reflect the business

Although the first goal – 'gain the trust of the business' – is essentially a question of customer-friendly management of the supply of IT capabilities, this second goal – 'understand and reflect the business' is the complement of the first: it's a question of dealing with demand management. At the same time, while our first goal is really about getting to grips with what's already in place, this second goal is about putting structures, communications and procedures in place which can begin to effectively shape and prioritise activity going forward in a way that really reflects business needs and priorities.

The key principles which apply in attaining this goal, as highlighted in Figure 9.2 are 'create a common language', 'foster relationships with key IT suppliers', 'manage IT as a business driven portfolio' and 'work towards coordinated goals and objectives'.

Start with a 'domain model' of business activity

The most fundamental activity which underpins the ability to understand and reflect the business is the creation of a high-level appreciation, shared by business and IT, of how the business activity can be partitioned into domains that are each driven by distinct sets of priorities and constraints, which affect how they should be supported by IT. This is the role of Enterprise Architecture (EA) practice, and it's the first thing you should start tackling to address this second goal. This is discussed within the 'create a common language' principle, but due to the central nature of EA to the whole of IT–business alignment, we also cover it in more detail in a dedicated section, later in this chapter.

Once you have started on the path of creating a 'domain model', you can then turn your attention to structuring current and planned IT activity into a portfolio of services (as outlined in the 'manage IT as a business-driven portfolio' principle).

Identify areas of misalignment

First of all you need to identify gaps, overlaps and incorrect work priorities in your set of current and planned IT services. Here, the set of business domains identified and characterised through Enterprise Architecture provides the framework. Overlaying your set of current and planned IT services on this domain model will highlight:

- Where priority areas for the business are not well served by current or future projects or services

- Where IT activities are being (or have been) delivered in a way that over or under delivers against business needs and expectations

- Where IT capabilities are replicated within different areas of the business, and so where opportunities for consolidation and de-duplication lie.

Balance the portfolio for overall business advantage

The outcome of this overlay process should be a map which illustrates some overall priorities for change if you are to really reflect business goals, concerns and priorities with the IT services that are provided. The next step is to work on refining this prioritisation using the portfolio definition approach outlined in the 'manage IT as a business-driven portfolio' principle.

In brief this is about categorising IT services and capabilities according to change strategies that make most sense in the business context. In the principle, we identify four strategies: 'maintain', 'improve', 'transform' and 'kill'. Real-world budget constraints mean that no matter how much you might like, it's impractical to embark on a radical transformation programme for every IT service that doesn't reflect the needs of the business domain in which it operates. This means it's important to balance effort, money and risk across the portfolio according to the overall priorities of the business.

Of course, doing this means communicating regularly and quite deeply with key business stakeholders. You'll need to address the issues outlined in Chapter 4 – specifically, 'avoiding technobabble' and 'language and the IT investment life cycle' – if you are to really get to the bottom of business priorities and create an alignment worklist that is fit for purpose.

A major challenge that you're bound to encounter at this point concerns balancing the portfolio in a way that is acceptable to the needs of the business stakeholder community as a whole, while still being practical. Budgets and time are not infinite, so it won't be possible to satisfy all the people all the time. Instead, the goal has to be to agree a programme of work that is really optimal for the business as a whole. Some stakeholders will appear to 'receive' more immediate benefit from the programme than others: the trick is in getting the whole community to see the bigger picture. We provide a number of tools to help you in this quest in the 'work towards coordinated goals and objectives' principle.

Drive supplier and internal capability management from the portfolio

It's easy to forget that even where you have a centralised IT organisation, there are other providers of IT services and capabilities that are equally important to bring into alignment. Technology tool, application and infrastructure suppliers and external service providers are essential parts of the equation, and any work that you do to identify, categorise and prioritise the elements of an alignment work plan must extend to them. We look at some ways to bring suppliers into the picture in the 'foster relationships with key IT suppliers' principle.

Equally, it's very easy to focus on the technological aspects of an alignment work programme (or indeed any change programme) and ignore the human factors – specifically, does the IT organisation have people within it with the right skills to enable the change? Specifically in this situation it's likely that communication, persuasion and networking skills may need attention, in addition to more technologically focused architecture, programme management and supplier management skills. Do you know what skills and resources the IT organisation really has at its disposal, beyond technical skills (e.g. the number of Java programmers you have)?

Goal 3: engage the business

The third of our four alignment goals – 'engage the business' – builds on the supply and demand management capabilities you create in reaching the first two goals, to build much closer connections between IT staff and business executives on a day-to-day basis, in order to create deeper mutual understanding of the constraints and capabilities that IT and business place on each other.

We describe the vehicle for this goal as 'service management in the business' because its central idea is that a set of IT representatives should be dedicated to working within business teams to help educate both sides about needs, demand for services and capabilities, sources for those services and capabilities, service constraints and so on. Crucially, as we explained in more detail in the 'establish a peer relationship between business and IT' principle, the scope of this 'service manager' role can't be bounded by discrete project phases, as it is with traditional business analysts; service managers are responsible and accountable for IT services throughout their lifecycles rather than diving in and out of business teams to gather project requirements.

The central role of the service manager

Service managers are, in effect, brokers of supply and demand, with the IT organisation just one supplier among many of IT capabilities to the business. The central role of the service manager in creating sustainable IT–business alignment means that it's vital, as we discussed in the 'establish a peer relationship between business and IT' principle, to invest time and money to ensure that service managers have the right mix of technical, analytical, business and interpersonal skills. Service managers have to understand business priorities, activities and processes as they are realised at the coal face of day-to-day business, as well as to be able to communicate back to the business all the relevant details concerning the combined ability of internal and external IT service providers to deliver results (or otherwise).

Service managers are also key players in the IT Governance Board process that we discussed in our 'work towards coordinated goals and objectives' principle, because they're in an unique position to be able to identify duplicated projects and work items, and consequent opportunities to develop shared service capabilities.

Service managers also play a vital role in supplier management because, through engagement with the business when service requirements are being defined and refined and when problems are being investigated, they can help influence IT supplier selection where technology purchasing is distributed across multiple teams (as it is in many organisations). In this kind of environment it's all too easy for the value of strategic supplier choices to be diluted by piecemeal 'off menu' selection by business executives. By helping the IT organisation consolidate licensing agreements and supplier relationships, service managers are therefore major potential contributors to overall IT cost and risk management activities. In practice, a common way to exert a standardising influence over supplier selection is to purchase enterprise license agreements with preferred suppliers centrally and then to prime service managers to influence how individual distributed project teams them – using a preferred supplier means the licenses are already paid for!

Suppliers provide more than just products

This process of engaging the business to discuss supplier relationships isn't just about constraining business choices. Sometimes it can work the other way around, providing greater insight into the value that suppliers may bring to the business beyond technology standardisation. For example, a business team may have chosen to engage with a particular IT supplier because the supplier is able to provide valuable best practice insight into how the business could be operating in its industry and geography. In this scenario, understanding the role of such a supplier helps to highlight the benchmark that the IT organisation and its 'strategic' suppliers have to reach, if these business teams are to really commit to the overall alignment programme.

Ongoing review of the business-driven portfolio

In order to ensure sustainability of the business driven portfolio approach, you have to make sure that it continues to reflect the reality of business on the ground as well as the strategic direction of the organisation. If business reality and the shape of the service portfolio diverge too much, the business will quickly become disillusioned with the overall process of 'working with IT', trust will diminish and engagement will be that much more difficult.

To insulate against divergence, you can institute a regular review process which keeps the portfolio up-to-date. Service managers play a key role here too, as they can drive the mechanics of the review process by surveying business executives and teams with stakes in the services they manage.

Engagement drives demand – architecture models are key

Of course, it's at this point – when the IT organisation seeks to get seriously integrated into the day-to-day workings of business teams – that questions of work prioritisation and triage become particularly pressing. As representatives from the IT organisation start to proactively engage to uncover work patterns and more obscure requirements, business teams become more open about their likes, dislikes and needs in terms of IT tools and services. This is likely to lead to a major jump in demand for service features and changes, and this demand surge needs to be managed carefully.

The EA process (as discussed in the 'create a common language' principle and also in some detail later in this chapter) is the key to smoothing out demand at times like this because the models that are created – and the process of business engagement involved in their creation – should help individual business executives and teams to understand the bigger picture and the practical implications of IT budget constraints.

Goal 4: drive the business

The last of our four goals represents the ultimate realisation of IT-business alignment: the situation where the IT organisation is in a position to not only respond to business demand in a timely and appropriate manner, but also drive changes in the business by effectively and consistently demonstrating the business opportunities associated with technology innovation.

The key principles which apply in attaining this goal, as highlighted in Figure 9.2 are 'create a common language', 'foster relationships with key IT suppliers', 'manage IT as a business-driven portfolio', 'work towards coordinated goals and objectives', and 'establish a peer relationship between business and IT'.

Governance and the CIO: defining the architecture for IT management

If 'IT governance' is about defining an architecture for IT management, as we believe it is, then it is at this point that the CIO starts to drive the scope of that architecture outwards, from an IT-focused view to a view which places responsibility and authority for IT outcomes on both IT and business teams. It's at this point in the alignment journey that CIOs can justifiably claim seats at the board tables in their organisations, start to make demands from the other management board representatives concerning ongoing business accountability for service delivery and start to open discussion of changes which are likely to affect IT service provision. Equally, it presents opportunities to outline how technology can facilitate and enable business change. We talk about this opportunity in more detail in our 'establish a peer relationship between business and IT' principle.

A very important enabler for the CIO to drive appropriate change and transformation in the business, is the ability for IT to feed back ideas to business leaders when it uncovers what appear to be problems. EA again plays a key role here (see the 'create a common language' principle). By explicitly modelling the links that exist between the business vision, mission and strategy, business activity areas and IT capabilities, EA models, as they are tested and developed, can themselves highlight areas where links are missing, poorly defined, not representative of reality and so on.

With the CIO in a senior organisational role, the IT organisation is in a position to use that modelling work to drive debate at senior levels within the business concerning how the business itself can identify and drive strategies more consistently. In this way the value of Enterprise Architecture work is not just about understanding IT's role within the business but it's also about using the understanding of how IT and business interact on a day-to-day basis, to understand disconnections between strategic business intent and business reality.

Taking a broader view of strategic suppliers

We've already made reference to the potential value of supplier relationships above and beyond the transfer of technology tools and products. Some of the largest IT suppliers – particularly those which have a strong history of delivering business application suites or strong consultancy capabilities – might be in a position to influence business executives where you are not.

You can use this to your advantage, rather than trying to battle against it (see our 'foster relationships with key IT suppliers' principle). You can work with your community of strategically aligned, critical IT suppliers to help drive an IT–business alignment agenda into the business if you're having trouble making that case yourself. These companies will have important industry insight and experience from working with other customers and are often taken more seriously as they're an external rather than an internal voice.

On a related note, driving *appropriate* change and transformation means that the IT organisation cannot be in the driving seat when it comes to defining business processes and practices. Indeed, sometimes it has to actively decide to take a back seat.

Sometimes IT and business teams will have to work side by side to define the best route forward, but at other times it makes sense for both IT and the business to defer expertise to a key IT supplier. This means actively looking to change how things are done in the business to support the best practices encoded in a supplier's offering. In business activity domains which can benefit from a high degree of repeatability and structured automation and where activity doesn't really differentiate the organisation from its competitors – those which are subject to regulatory compliance are good candidates — it makes absolute sense to buy practices and processes off the shelf, in the technology product, rather than the other way around.

The central role of Enterprise Architecture

As we're sure you will have noticed, the concept of Enterprise Architecture (EA) crops up time and again in our discussion of the six principles for IT–business alignment, and also in our explanation of the chain of four alignment goals. The importance of this capability to delivering sustainable IT–business alignment can't be overstated.

There are two main ways in which the practice of EA contributes towards the chain of four alignment goals and the six alignment principles – it's a competence which has truly strategic weight.

First of all, as we discuss in the 'create a common language' principle, the process of conducting EA work itself engages business stakeholders in discussion about how the business works and how IT supports business activities, and so helps to promote common understanding.

Secondly, the outputs of the EA process create a domain-based view of how IT supports the business and how this can be optimised, that in turn drives:

- How organisations develop and manage business-driven IT service portfolios
- How they triage and reconcile conflicting work request
- The roles that strategic IT suppliers should play in delivering and contributing towards IT services

The outputs can even direct the path of the overall alignment programme, something we discuss in more detail in Agile alignment below.

As we mentioned in the Chapter 1, it's vital to remember that although EA can look at first sight rather like the enterprise-wide business modelling exercises of old that invariably took months or years, then stalled and failed to deliver value, if it's pursued in a pragmatic, incremental and business-driven way, real value can be delivered.

The scope of EA

As Figure 9.3 shows, for EA programmes to be really successful in bringing IT and business closer together, they have to be influenced by and influence, a wide range of key

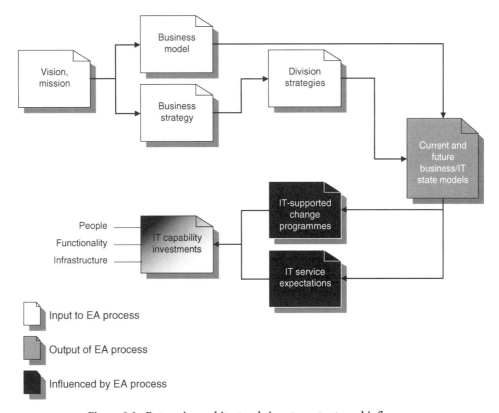

Figure 9.3: Enterprise architecture's inputs, outputs and influences

business and IT management anchors – all the way from business vision and mission statements, to IT capability investment projects.

EA inputs

In order to effectively enable sustainable IT–business alignment EA has to take its inputs from a mixture of existing strategy and management artefacts, both business and IT related:

- *Vision and mission statements*: most organisations (certainly large ones) have forma-lised vision and mission statements, which seek to crystallise the aspirations of the executive team in terms of the effect that the organisation will have on its customers, market and possibly society in general. These statements are useful inputs to the EA process because, if they are doing their job properly, they should offer very clear signposts to anyone evaluating a strategic decision – is this the kind of thing that the organisation should do? – and so provide an analytical context for the business model and strategy.

- *Business model and business strategy*: the organisation's business model might not be formally written down – many aren't. If it's not, we suggest that someone works on this straight away! There are many different interpretations of the information that should comprise a business model definition, but at the very least a business model definition should include information about the organisation's products and services; its customers; how it reaches those customers (in terms of sales, marketing and distribution); the main skills and capabilities it needs to operate; how costs will be structured; and how money will be made. The business strategy should then describe the ways in which an organisation aims to realise its vision and mission, taking into account the context of the environment it operates in (competitive, regulatory and so on) and local resource constraints (budgets, skills and so on). Business model and strategy documentation are key inputs to the EA process because together they provide the major signposts for the alignment of IT capabilities with business needs.

- *Divisional strategies*: often, particularly in large organisations, strategy-setting power is heavily devolved to divisional stakeholders, with the result that each stakeholder has his or her own priorities which might conflict with those of others. Divisional strategy documentation, where relevant, is a key input to the EA process because it will suggest ways that architectural principles might need to be partitioned into separate domains – each with its own drivers and priorities (see our *Manage IT as a business-driven portfolio* principle for more detail on this).

- *Existing IT capability investments*: this is where a lot of EA efforts start out: doing what some refer to as 'bottom-up' EA modelling, documenting the existing technology landscape. It's not surprising that EA efforts so often start out here because most EA activity is carried out by people with technology backgrounds. However, the risk with a heavily bottom-up approach that doesn't also include a review of other key business focused inputs (outlined above) is that the business focused inputs should, by rights, have a lot of influence over how the EA process as a whole proceeds. It makes sense, for example, to focus documentation efforts on IT landscape areas where the business strategy and model imply that a lot of change is going to occur.

It's important to realise that all these inputs will change in form and in content over time. For this reason EA can't be a one-shot process: it has to be an ongoing, continuous programme of work with regular review cycles. Involvement of key business stakeholders throughout, from the initial work and including the regular reviews, is critical.

EA outputs

The principal outputs of an EA process are variations on a theme: models which document the business activities that are carried out in the organisation, and how

IT capabilities and services support those activities. An effective EA programme needs to be responsible for creating and maintaining two sets of models:

- *'As-is' models*: these document how business activities and IT capabilities relate in practice, at the time the EA work is done.

- *'To-be' models*: these document the relationships between business activities and IT capabilities in a future state where IT services are more closely aligned with business needs.

These models work well when their foundation is a description, which is comprehensible as broadly as possible, by both business and IT people. Two examples of approaches which do a good job here are Microsoft's Motion methodology and IBM's Component Business Modelling methodology. Both use variants of the same idea: logical functional models that illustrate, at a high level, the main business capabilities that exist within the organisation; and then use those as a framework for mapping IT capabilities against business needs.

One of the most important factors which will determine the degree of real business value that flows from your EA initiative is how the 'future state', as documented in 'to-be' EA models is arrived at.

It's entirely possible, if an EA team is not properly grounded in business reality, for the future state that they aim for to be almost entirely dictated by 'what's some really cool technology that we could get involved in deploying?' This is an extreme example, but there are many cases where EA initiatives have failed to deliver value because the future state being aimed for is fundamentally mismatched with the direction that the business is going in. For this reason it's crucial that the EA team is plugged in, directly or indirectly, to the processes that determine business and IT goals and objectives. We discuss this in more detail in *EA process: ivory towers vs consensus building*, in Chapter 4.

EA influences

The process of EA yields some vital assistance in creating a common language for IT and business, if it's done right, but the value of EA primarily comes from its role in influencing the direction of IT investment and delivery. It's vital to understand the scope of the influence that EA should ideally have. Just as some organisations misunderstand EA as primarily being a 'scale thing', some organisations also see EA as primarily guiding software development activity, but this is wrong. EA should have an influence in three related areas:

- *IT change programmes*: in this capacity EA is an influencer in the pursuit of our fourth alignment goal, 'drive the business', which is all about driving appropriate change and transformation. IT change programmes tend to have a life of their own, and EA's challenge is to try and ensure that changes move the organisation incrementally in the right direction. In truth, these programmes are influenced heavily by a broad and broadening community of business stakeholders, and EA teams typically have to work hard (we suggest through direct or indirect participation in an IT Governance Board process) to balance the forces which are the defining aspects of planned programmes.

- *IT service expectations*: in this capacity EA is an influencer in the pursuit of our third alignment goal, 'engage the business', which is all about implementing service management directly within business teams. The breadth of EA's remit must consider operational issues as well as the procurement/development phases of the IT life cycle. If EA is really going to help enable sustainable IT–business alignment, it can't focus only on ensuring that things get built in a way that moves the organisation's IT footprint closer to a desired 'to-be' state. Up to 80% of the lifetime costs of IT systems are incurred after their initial rollout, so it's ludicrous to have EA efforts stop short of getting involved with the operational implications of architectural principles and policies. As more and more IT organisations seek to rationalise their portfolios and move towards the use of shared services to improve cost, risk and quality, EA teams actively influencing multiple projects and programmes are in an ideal position to help individual project teams understand the likely operational demands that will be placed on systems as they roll out and as other projects come on stream.

- *IT capability investments*: in this capacity EA is an influencer in the pursuit of our second alignment goal, 'understand and reflect the business', which is all about managing demand for IT service and shaping the delivery of services so that they reflect business priorities. It's common for EA practice to focus on influencing (and being influenced by) the functionality of business systems and the IT infrastructure that underpins them. But EA teams should also work to understand the skill implications of moving in a particular direction and raise awareness of those skill implications to individual project teams and to the IT management team as necessary. Too often grand migration or investment plans are drawn up, and the skill implications of those plans become apparent only once work starts in earnest.

Finding the right level for EA modelling

Lastly, if EA is going to have real value, it can't be just applied to capabilities that get built by internal IT development teams. Your internal IT organisation is likely to be only one IT service provider among many, so the intelligence gathered through the EA process needs to be applied equally across all services, including those that aren't delivered in-house by a central IT department.

The consequence for this, of course, is that EA models have to be pitched at a level of abstraction that can apply equally across internally delivered and externally delivered services. It makes no sense to drive architecture work to a level of detail that is irrelevant in the context of infrastructure, application or business process services supplied by outside parties.

The phrase to keep in mind here is 'just enough is just right'.

Modelling alignment: domains, business processes and services

In our 'manage IT as a business-driven portfolio' principle, we've already explained why it makes sense to apply the concept of 'domains' to partition business activity. Different domains group together areas of related activity that share similar business characteristics – in terms of priorities, operational qualities and operational constraints, for example. Individual domains of business activity then shape the way in which IT services should provide support to the business.

We've also talked briefly about the two core conceptual elements that are particularly suited to the kinds of EA output models we should be creating for today's businesses: business processes and managed IT services. But why do we think these are such suitable candidate concepts?

Business processes

Earlier in this book, in Chapter 2, we explained how, to make themselves more competitive and in tune with customer needs, organisations are looking to make their core business processes more open and responsive – configuring them to be driven directly by demand, rather than by supply. We also saw that organisations are looking to systematise how they foster innovation – not just in terms of innovation in the products and services they offer, but also in terms of how they're structured and how they operate. And we discussed how they're looking beyond traditional innovation sources to consider how they can work with their own employees and suppliers, partners, academia and customers (or citizens) to uncover and realise innovations.

In line with this set of business changes, we explained how the focus of business automation has moved from the back office to the 'front office', and beyond, to the connections between organisations. More and more, organisations are looking to differentiate themselves using combinations of capabilities that span different functions, divisions and teams, and IT drivers are changing as a result.

When you also factor in the moves that organisations take to outsource 'non-core' capabilities in more sophisticated ways, it should be clear that the traditional ways of documenting and analysing business capabilities – most of which have worked from the starting points of organisational charts or financial 'charts of accounts' – aren't suitable for today's business world. Organisational boundaries (both internal and external) are changing more quickly, and the lines between them are increasingly fuzzy.

In this context, the concept of the *business process* offers the most appropriate basis for describing and analysing business activities. The suitability of business process as a concept is boosted by the fact that in IT circles today, through the Business Process

Management (BPM) movement, modelling and automation of business processes directly in software is once again a key goal.

Managed services

Along with the use of business process as the concept for describing and analysing business activities, we need a concept that can capture the perspective that we need on IT capabilities and their support for business operations in today's environment.

The concept of managed IT services provides a firm foundation for describing IT capabilities and support for business operations, for five reasons:

- The concept of 'service' is well understood in business circles.

- The concept of 'service orientation' as a paradigm for delivering IT capabilities is becoming well understood in IT circles too.

- Service-oriented approaches to IT capability delivery are increasingly being pursued in IT organisations in parallel with Business Process Management initiatives.

- The concept of 'IT service' is also well understood in business circles, as organisations become more familiar with shared-services-based sourcing strategies.

- The concept of 'managed service' sets aspirations and expectations within the IT organisation that the delivery of IT capabilities that have real business value isn't just about designing and building systems – it's about managing the whole lifecycle of systems, from 'cradle' to 'grave'. Thinking about, and organising IT teams for, 'managed service delivery' explicitly forces together development and operational administration disciplines to collaborate in the delivery of capabilities in the context of well-understood contracts that are also business-meaningful.

This last point isn't just of theoretical interest: it's a crucial tool in building a common language for business and IT. Today, it's a rare thing for IT organisations to be able to offer any continuity in how they interact with business project sponsors throughout the lifecycle of an investment.

As the left-hand side of Figure 9.4 shows, today a typical investment discussion is very coarse-grained: the conversation between business and IT is typically at the level of a 'system' or an application – a coarse-grained IT capability. When it comes to operating the investment after it's been procured or developed, however, the type of discussion changes radically. If a business sponsor wants information about the performance of the investment they've made, all that the IT organisation can do is point to fine-grained evidence: server uptime, database performance and so on. When it comes to attempting to manage change to that investment, things get even more complicated – it's difficult to work out what the discussion should refer to, which would make sense to both the IT side and the business side. The common result from this lack of continuity means that it's very

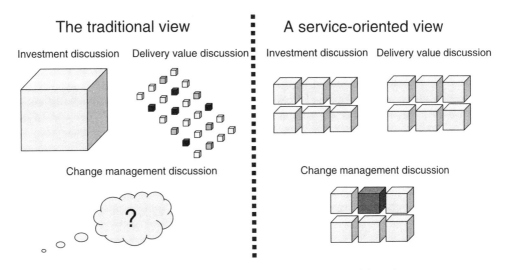

Figure 9.4: Service: a common concept across the life cycle

difficult for IT 'customers' to equate what has been delivered with what they might have anticipated, which leads to lack of visibility and a lack of trust.

The concept of 'managed services' has the great benefit, as the right-hand side of Figure 9.4 shows, of being equally suitable for investment discussions ('we need to invest in a set of services that provide A, B and C'); delivery discussions ('A and B are working very well, but demand for C is outstripping the capacity we built for it') and change discussions ('the real change focus should be service B').

Domain models and shared services

In our principle 'manage IT as a business-driven portfolio' and also in this chapter we explain why it makes sense to partition business activity into discrete domains, and then target IT services at those domains in a way that tunes service delivery to the particular needs of each business activity domain. But at the same time, in our 'work towards coordinated goals and objectives' principle we explicitly recognise the drive to deliver more shared services as a way to consolidate and rationalise IT spending and effort.

How can you pursue these two apparently conflicting initiatives? The answer is to create one or more IT service domains that are not tied to specific business activity domains but which 'house' shared IT services.

A key question remains, however and that concerns what services are feasible to share across a variety of business activities. For if the domain-based model for IT-business alignment tells us anything, it's that not all business activities need the same kind of support from IT services. Each business activity domain has its own imperatives and optimisations, and thus it is going to be subject to its own 'change forces'.

What this means for delivering shared services is that you need to be very careful about implementing shared services that will potentially be consumed in support of multiple business activity domains. Change forces are likely to act in different ways and at different rates across a set of business domains consuming IT services in this way, and the likely outcome will be unsustainable.

A guideline is therefore to stick to defining shared services for what can genuinely be thought of as infrastructure – that is, 'horizontal' technical capabilities that are universally applicable, such as security and identity management, auditing, print, web serving and so on. Alternatively it can make sense to define shared services which will be consumed in multiple places within one business activity domain. It might be possible to define shared services that are consumed across a set of business activity domains – but only if those domains themselves share similar business goals, priorities, optimisations and constraints.

Agile alignment

You're probably aware by now that creating sustainable IT–business alignment in your organisation is a nontrivial project. Depending on where your organisation is in terms of its current maturity and capability in the context of our four alignment goals, it's likely to take months, if not years, to really get the changes you will need to make ingrained into working practices and behaviours.

The first of our four goals – 'gain the trust of the business' – is the goal likely to take the most effort because to really get into a position where the IT organisation can consistently deliver a set of business-meaningful services and also provide business-meaningful feedback on them and the costs involved in their delivery, This will take significant investment in tools, processes and skills. Trying to do this all in one go, across the whole of the IT organisation, is going to be very difficult indeed.

At the end of the day, sustainability isn't just a matter of putting strategies and structures in place to anticipate and manage change flexibly; it's also a matter of not biting off more than you can chew in a kind of 'big bang' transformation, which will probably raise unrealistic expectations and then fail to deliver. A sustainable outcome from your IT–business alignment initiative demands an incremental approach which yields visible results quickly.

Getting started

Bootstrapping IT-business alignment

The alternative to a 'big bang' transformation, of course, is to identify priority areas for work and focus on them initially – focus on the application of our alignment principles to high-priority IT initiatives, and then work incrementally to apply the principles to new initiatives as they come along.

But how can you reliably identify high-priority initiatives? One of the characteristics of misaligned IT and business is that priorities are often skewed – either by a predilection on the IT side for the application of a particular new technology or tool; or by a bias in one or more lines-of-business for 'pet projects' sponsored by powerful executives.

What this means is that in order to bootstrap alignment, you have to first of all embark on an initial piece of lightweight EA work in order to uncover one or two domains of business activity where needs are particularly pressing and where IT capabilities are currently poorly positioned to provide the right kind of support.

Get organisational structures in place

Throughout our six alignment principles we've introduced a number of different orga- nisational structures and bodies, and it's worth revisiting them here because you'll need to get them in place and working in order to move from pursuing one alignment goal to the next. The three key focuses for your organisational work are as follows:

- An IT Governance Board, involving input from key stakeholders across the IT organisa- tion and lines of business, a representative enterprise architect and service managers

- An Enterprise Architecture team (or a role, if your organisation isn't large enough to warrant a dedicated team) with the authority to work across the organisation as a whole

- A Service Management team (or a role, if as above your organisation isn't large enough to warrant a dedicated team) where individuals work within individual business teams to drive two-way conversations about the relationship between business activity and IT services 'at the coal face'.

All these organisational changes are likely to need to be supported with training for the individuals taking part. To work out who is a good fit for these roles, you need to carry out an honest skills audit that focuses not on the technical capabilities of individuals within the IT organisation but on their interpersonal and management capabilities. It makes sense to get an outside specialist to help you do this. Then, you can sponsor tailored training for the suitable candidates. Where such candidates don't exist, you will have to make the case for recruitment.

It's vital that IT governance, Enterprise Architecture and service management roles are seen as positions that have a valuable contribution to make and that they're sought after by talented individuals. If these roles are seen as quiet corners where troublemakers are put, you'll end up with poor performance in critical areas, and the whole alignment initiative will falter.

Tuning your approach

This year two of the big IT industry analyst firms – Gartner Group and Forrester Research – have released research papers advising clients that they need to aim to create IT organisations that conform to one of three archetypes. Forrester identifies 'solid utilities', 'trusted suppliers', and 'partner players'; Gartner identifies 'IT utilities', 'IT services brokers' and 'business change agents'.

Unsurprisingly, our research has identified a similar set of roles that IT organisations can play – and indeed these correspond to our chain of four alignment goals.

But just because we have presented a chain of four goals for sustainable IT–business alignment, as we explained earlier, it does not mean that every organisation should aspire to move itself completely to be able to 'drive the business'. Sometimes this isn't warranted.

The *really* crucial thing to understand is that in *every* organisation this is not a matter of 'either-or'. Our research has shown us that *every* organisation carries out activities where IT absolutely can and should play a proactive role in identifying and driving change. And at the same time, every organisation carries out activities where IT's role is best constrained to being a passive provider of services under the control of lines of business.

Different domains, different balance of effort

In our view of the world as laid out in this book, this means that different domains of business activity should drive you to place different balances of effort across the four alignment goals.

As Figure 9.5 below illustrates, in domains where activity is highly structured, mature, and where the overall business driver is cost management, it probably makes sense to focus the bulk of alignment effort on the first two of our four alignment goals – 'gain the trust of the business' and 'understand and reflect the business'.

By contrast, in domains where business activity really contributes to business differentiation and particularly where activity needs to be strongly coordinated across traditional business functional silos for strategies to succeed, it will make sense to shift the balance of effort slightly so that proportionally more effort is focused on pushing towards our third and fourth goals – 'engage the business' and 'drive the business'.

Managing for continual change

We called this book 'The Technology Garden' because a single observation about the nature of IT in business led us to want to write this book.

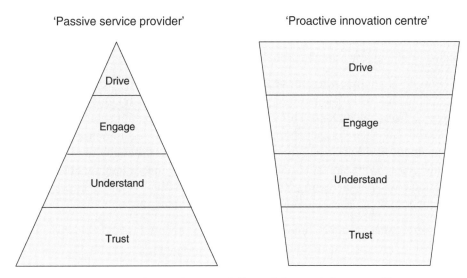

'Passive service provider'   'Proactive innovation centre'

Figure 9.5: Different domains, different balance of alignment effort

The observation is this: it's a folly to give advice about managing IT and IT portfolios as if they were engineering products like cars, bridges or buildings. In reality, organisations' IT portfolios are ever-growing, ever-changing – and in reality, they can't really be controlled. They're much more like gardens than they are like buildings. And it's impossible to turn a garden into a building – no matter how hard you try.

What this means is that unless you work for a pretty small organisation, and even if you're a CIO at the top of the organisation and at the top of your game, you can't control IT completely. The most you can do is put structures, procedures, skills and relationships in place that keep the natural tendency towards disorder under a degree of control and which continually edge the organisation as a whole towards a more effective future.

A 'four seasons' approach to governance

In some business activity domains, where innovation needs to be pursued and fostered, it makes sense to apply relatively 'light touch' control to the selection of suppliers and technologies, the design of solutions, the definition of operational procedures for services and so on. But this kind of approach should be applied to a minority of initiatives. And vitally, every initiative where the rules are relaxed should be clearly identified to all involved (particularly to the IT Governance Board).

Where things get particularly interesting is where initiatives shift from domain to domain over time.

We all know that change doesn't just happen at the level of technologies, platforms, applications and services, but happens at the level of business activities and their

IT support needs. What's important to realise is that in terms of our domain model concept, business activities – and IT services that support them – can also migrate between domains, or at the very least the domains they live in can morph.

One example of an area where business activity can remain structurally the same but change its business role, priority and goals, is the airline industry and its move to offer customer self-service check-in. This was a differentiating capability among airlines for a short period. But then, in a few months, it moved into a nondifferentiating capability for the majority of the airlines. Minor innovations, such as the ability to print your own boarding card at home, are still occurring, but primarily the airlines are now motivated by reducing costs and increasing efficiency rather than differentiating themselves from their competitors.

Another interesting example comes from the area of loyalty card scheme management, highlighted in a recent paper from McKinsey[1] consultancy:

> *'Many retailers, for example, now combine data from loyalty cards and transactions to understand the individual consumer's buying patterns. As a result, the collection, storage and analysis of transaction data – once clearly "scale" functions* [functions that were optimised by the IT organisation to be reliable and scalable above all else] *– have become a competitive weapon and should be governed for business alignment* [where change needs to be driven jointly by IT and lines of business].'

With the ability of business activity to fundamentally change its role and contribution to overall business value – sometimes moving from 'innovation and competitive differentiation' to 'standard activity that just needs to work' and sometimes moving the other way – we talk to clients about the importance of creating an approach to IT governance and IT–business alignment that is 'seasonal'. We highlight four modes of operation, each of which corresponds to a different phase in the long-term lifecycle of IT services:

- In the 'spring' mode of operation, the approach to governing investment should be to sow the seeds for innovative application of IT. It may well be that this innovation is conducted outside any formal or centralised IT organisation, and in this mode, it makes no sense to force a change of location.

- In the 'summer' mode of operation, the approach to governing innovative investment should be to let those seeds grow – monitoring activity (through service managers) and relevantly influencing the use of IT to maximise the ability for innovation initiatives to integrate with other IT services and structures in an efficient way.

---

[1]*Managing for scale, speed and innovation*, S. Marwaha and P. Willmott, *McKinsey on IT - Fall 2006 issue*

- In the 'autumn' mode of operation, the approach should be focused on 'harvesting' those innovative investments that are now starting to become established enablers of mainstream business activity. Where this kind of domain transition is ready to take place, the IT leadership needs to proactively take charge of the initiative and put change programme in place to reengineer parts of the initiative (if required). The usual procedure for debating, agreeing and prioritising this investment within IT Governance Board should be pursued.

- The 'winter' mode of operation is all about planning – working IT–business relationships to uncover potential areas for innovation investment, researching potentially relevant new technologies, tools or approaches and so on.

Socialising change

We can't leave this chapter without a discussion of some tools and tactics that you can use to help improve the chances of changes being accepted, within IT teams and within the organisation as a whole. Change management isn't all or even mostly about project management; a huge part of the battle is in managing people's expectations and fears and motivating them to accept and champion the change.

We want to call out two tools in particular: RACI charts, which help to identify the stakeholders in a particular initiative, and stakeholder communication plans, which help to identify the most effective way of reaching different stakeholders and ensuring that they buy into potential changes.

RACI charts – identifying stakeholders

For each significant change in your alignment initiative – particularly for any change which involves a significant shift in responsibilities, authority or status within the IT organisation – you need to be completely aware of the different parties that have a stake in such a change taking place and what their roles will be as the change project progresses.

As shown in Figure 9.6, RACI charts (sometimes called RASCI charts) are a useful tool to help you identify and classify stakeholders according to their role and impact. As the name suggests there are five role types:

- The person who is **R**esponsible for driving the change. There should be only one of these. If no one has been identified, or if there are potentially multiple owners, this is a red flag and needs to be dealt with immediately

- The person who the responsible individual is **A**ccountable to – typically this person is the approver of the change

- A role or group that can be **S**upportive – by providing resources or insight

MyCo Alignment initiative – Phase 1

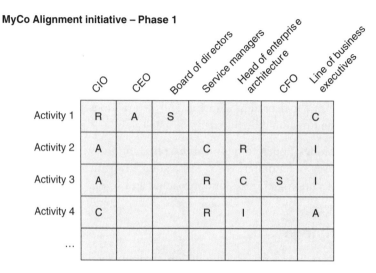

	CIO	CEO	Board of directors	Service managers	Head of enterprise architecture	CFO	Line of business executives
Activity 1	R	A	S				C
Activity 2	A			C	R		I
Activity 3	A			R	C	S	I
Activity 4	C			R	I		A
...							

Figure 9.6: An example RACI chart

- A role or group that must be **C**onsulted – because they have information or capabilities, or perhaps for political reasons needed to make the change succeed

- A role or group that must be **I**nformed – people who 'need to know', but who don't need to be consulted

Stakeholder communication plans

Once you've used a RACI chart to work through a set of key activities in your alignment initiative and identify the different types of stakeholders who will play a role in implementing

Change activity 3.5 – Create Service Manager Roles

Stakeholder	Role (R,A,C,I)	Fears	Opportunities	Communication plan
Technology managers	C	Does this mean my role is less important? Am I going to be outsourced?	Focus on developing technology skills without business distractions	Workshop with all Technology Managers to allow group debate and dialogue; one to one meetings with TMs to hear individual concerns
CEO	A	Is this going to create more overhead and just slow us down?	Clear day-to-day pathway linking business needs to IT capabilities	Survey line of business executives and report regularly on progress
New service managers	C	Am I going to be able to do this job?	Valuable management role with great prospects	Individual meetings with new Service Managers and HR to develop personalised training plans
...	...	...	...	...

Figure 9.7: An example stakeholder communication plan

change, it pays to drill a little deeper and analyse how changes can best be communicated to stakeholders if they are to be won over.

Figure 9.7 shows a sample of a stakeholder communication plan, which can help you do this. Its chief role is to do nothing more than to make you put yourself in the shoes of the individuals and groups who might have something to fear, something to gain or both from the change – and then think about how you can best manage those fears and expectations.

Appendix

IT–business alignment scorecard toolkit

About the alignment scorecard

It was very important to us in writing this book that we created something that was really actionable, rather than just being an 'interesting read'. With that in mind, we've created a set of scorecard tools, based on the alignment framework set out in chapter 9, that you can use to support the implementation and monitoring of an IT–business alignment improvement programme. You can use the metrics that result from the scorecard to establish an initial baseline against which you can set targets for improvement and review progress on a regular (we recommend quarterly) basis.

The goals and metrics outlined are based on the four high-level goals described in chapter 9 and provide a starting point for understanding and assessment that we anticipate will be useful for most organisations looking to improve IT–business alignment. As with all such techniques, however, we can only provide a generic starting point. It may be appropriate to modify or extend the contents to reflect your circumstances.

The structure of the scorecard toolkit is deliberately simple, so assessments do not become an onerous activity.

Structure and use of the scorecard toolkit

Within this section you will find four 'Alignment Goal Rating Sheets' relating to the four main 'Applying the principles' goals, followed by a 'Scorecard Summary and Planning Sheet'.

The nature of the questions is such that assessments may need to be carried out in collaboration with representatives from the business, either individually or as a broader survey. Again, we would recommend that such activities are included as part of an overall improvement programme.

Using copies of the sheets, the procedure for carrying out an initial assessment or subsequent review is as follows:

- Work through the questions on each of the four rating sheets (20 questions in all) circling the score next to the response that matches your current situation. Don't worry if you cannot see an option that is an exact match, just select the one that is closest.

- Once all the questions have been answered, transfer the scores to the 'Scorecard Summary and Planning Sheet', putting them into the appropriate positions.

- Total the subgoal scores for each of the four main goals, and enter these into the *Total* boxes; then add up all four totals to derive the *overall IT–business alignment score* at the bottom of the sheet.

You will note that there are spaces on the scorecard summary sheet to identify key improvement initiatives and to set improvement targets that will be worked towards for the next review point. We urge you to use these spaces to think about what kind of improvements are achievable, and make commitments (if only to yourself). The target and historical information will be available to help determine progress in subsequent assessments.

Interpreting the scores

The primary value of a scorecard approach is that it allows a rapid and effective assessment of relative capability and/or progress across the defined goals and objectives. By comparing scores from different elements, it is easy to spot areas of relative strength and weakness, which should be used to set improvement priorities. In addition, it allows progress to be tracked over time by comparing the scores for each element between reviews.

For those wishing a more absolute interpretation, here is a mapping of the overall alignment score to the state of IT–business alignment, described in more qualitative terms:

Overall alignment score	Qualitative interpretation
80–100	The level of alignment between IT and the business is excellent. While it may be appropriate to improve in the few areas of shortfall (as identified in the scorecard), this probably amounts to tuning activities. The overall priority must be to maintain the alignment that currently exists.
60–80	While the IT organisation is doing a good job of supporting the business, significant areas of underperformance exist, and business management is therefore likely to have certain concerns with the operation and delivery of the IT organisation. The priority is to address those areas in which scores are low, prioritising activity in order of the goals, that is, 'Gain trust from the business first'. For example, if there are some basic issues that need resolving to gain the trust of the business, then deal with those first.
40–60	The chances are that IT is perceived by the business as not performing particularly well. We would anticipate that the business lacks trust in the IT organisation as a result of some major shortfalls in how IT services are delivered to the business. As above, the priority is to address those areas in which scores are low, prioritising activity in goal order.
Less than 40	The IT organisation is essentially dysfunctional. The recommendation is to put an improvement programme in place as a priority, making sure key personnel acquaint themselves with the principles in this book as part of the scoping and preparation process.

So, wondering where your IT organisation is on this spectrum? Just turn the page and start your assessment.

Alignment goal rating sheet

1

Gain trust from the business

Aim to be seen as a trusted supplier of IT services that 'just work'

Establish a clear two-way dialogue between IT and the business	
How do businesspeople perceive the way in which the IT organisation communicates with them?	
Option	*Score*
Clearly and openly at all levels	5
Clearly and openly via management and its nominated 'representatives'	4
Openly, but often struggles to understand clearly and/or be listened to	3
Clearly, but in a closed or defensive manner	2
Unclearly in a closed or defensive manner	1
Question not considered relevant	0

Align expectations of basic service delivery between IT and the business	
How well are expectations on service and project delivery aligned with the business?	
Option	*Score*
Expectations fully aligned, with mutually acceptable targets/SLAs where appropriate	5
Expectations aligned in most areas, moving towards alignment in others	4
Expectations aligned in most areas, but some significant sticking points remain	3
Significant misalignment, with many points of disagreement	2
No real attempt to align expectations as yet	1
Question not considered relevant	0

Achieve an acceptable level of availability and performance for all key services
How well are key services delivered and/or are improvement plans defined?

Option	Score
All key services are delivered to an acceptable level	5
Mostly acceptable with improvement plans in place to close the gap	4
Mostly acceptable with improvement plans yet to be formulated	3
Mostly unacceptable, but improvement plans in place	2
Mostly unacceptable, with improvement plans yet to be formulated	1
Question not considered relevant	0

Deliver new service capability in line with agreed commitments and expectations
How reliable is the IT organisation in delivering projects on time and to budget?

Option	Score
The great majority (>80%) deliver on time and within budget	5
The great majority are delivered on time, but they are often over budget or incomplete	4
The great majority come in within budget, but delivery is often late	3
Most (>50%) are delivered late and over budget	2
The great majority (>80%) are delivered late and over budget	1
Question not considered relevant	0

Implement effective measurement and feedback mechanisms
To what degree is the performance of IT monitored and reviewed via business meaningful metrics?

Option	Score
Comprehensive business meaningful metrics defined and fully reviewed with the business	5
Comprehensive business meaningful metrics defined and selectively reviewed with the business	4
Selective business meaningful metrics are defined and reported to the business	3
Selective business meaningful metrics are defined but are used only within the IT organisation	2
Business meaningful metrics are generally not used to track IT performance	1
Question not considered relevant	0

Alignment goal rating sheet

2

Understand and reflect the business

Deliver differentiated business support from IT

Establish mechanisms to coordinate goals and objectives *How does IT and the business make sure goals and objectives are coordinated?*	
Option	*Score*
Strategic executive level dialogue plus enterprise architecture practice (or equivalent)	5
Enterprise architecture practice (or equivalent) supported by senior IT management	4
More selective programme management or steering groups for specific initiatives	3
Ad hoc coordination on an 'as needed' basis	2
Little coordination beyond responding to requests from the business on a case-by-case basis	1
Question not considered relevant	0

Provide clear business context for significant IT-related activity *To what degree is IT-related activity mapped onto documented business domains?*	
Option	*Score*
Complete mapping across the entire range of IT activities	5
Mapping for particularly important or critical services and initiatives only	4
Mapping only for significant new initiatives or projects requiring business buy-in	3
Loose mapping for new projects and initiatives, but not formally documented	2
No real mapping of IT activity onto business domains	1
Question not considered relevant	0

Map the dependencies between assets, services and business value
How complete is your business-driven IT investment portfolio?

Option	Score
Fully populated from high-level domains and services down to low-level assets	5
Complete at a high-level, with detail present for key services only	4
Complete at a high-level, but with little detail as yet below this	3
A significant amount of low-level detail but yet to be mapped onto the higher-level view	2
No real concept of a business-driven portfolio at this moment in time	1
Question not considered relevant	0

Balance assets and services to deliver overall business advantage
How well balanced and optimised is your business-driven IT investment portfolio?

Option	Score
In place and fully optimised, it just needs maintaining	5
Most/all services evaluated with gaps and adjustments identified and optimisation in progress	4
Currently in the process of evaluating the portfolio in preparation for optimisation	3
Still in the process of populating the portfolio, not in a position to evaluate yet	2
No real concept of a business-driven IT portfolio at this moment in time	1
Question not considered relevant	0

Identify key IT suppliers
Have key suppliers been identified according to an objective assessment of criticality and contribution?

Option	Score
All key suppliers identified based on their criticality and contribution	5
Strategic suppliers identified, but other key suppliers not yet tied down	4
Candidate key suppliers identified but not yet qualified according to objective criteria	3
Have a working list of important suppliers, but this is not based on any objective assessment	2
No real view of which suppliers are important to us	1
Question not considered relevant	0

Alignment goal rating sheet

3

Engage the business

Implement IT service management *within* the business

Make IT an integral part of the business management agenda	
How well can business managers articulate IT-related plans or activities as they relate to their domain?	
Option	*Score*
The great majority (80%) of business managers can articulate this confidently and precisely	5
Those impacted by IT change programs can articulate precisely, others in general terms	4
The great majority are IT aware but can only articulate relevant plans in general terms	3
Some managers are aware and can articulate plans in general terms, but many cannot	2
Business managers are generally not aware of IT plans in anything other than vague terms	1
Question not considered relevant	0

Integrate IT service management into the business itself	
To what degree has service management been embedded into the business?	
Option	*Score*
Dedicated service managers are in place for all key parts of the business	5
Service managers are there for some parts of the business, other mechanisms elsewhere	4
Other mechanisms such as liaison representatives and steering groups broadly used	3
Other formal mechanisms are used in some areas but not others	2
There is no formal mechanism for integrating service management into the business	1
Question not considered relevant	0

Implement a balanced business approach to demand management
How do you ensure that IT resources are applied in a balanced way across the business?

Option	Score
There is a formal IT governance board in place	5
Service managers are in place and coordinate with each other to ensure ongoing balance	4
IT management arbitrates to resolve potential imbalances using the portfolio as a reference	3
IT management arbitrates in line with other points of reference, for example, existing budgets and plans	2
There is no real mechanism for ensuring balance	1
Question not considered relevant	0

Embrace key IT suppliers strategically and operationally
To what degree are key suppliers involved in business-related discussions?

Option	Score
Strategically and operationally, so we can benefit fully from their industry/domain expertise	5
We take their advice on operational matters but rarely involve them in strategic discussions	4
Key suppliers are invited to discuss business issues on an exceptional basis only	3
There is no formal involvement of key suppliers, but they do participate informally	2
As a general rule, we do not discuss business issues at all with IT suppliers	1
Question not considered relevant	0

Institutionalise the process of sustaining alignment
How do you ensure IT activities remain in alignment with business priorities?

Option	Score
Our business-driven portfolio is reviewed on a continuous basis	5
Our business-driven portfolio is reviewed on a periodic basis, for example, quarterly	4
Activities are reviewed against priorities via management meetings, steering groups, and so on	3
Major projects and initiatives are tracked against plan, but little alignment activity beyond this	2
No real mechanism to sustain alignment on an ongoing basis	1
Question not considered relevant	0

Alignment goal rating sheet

4

Drive the business

Appropriate change and transformation

Embrace IT as a strategic business enabler	
What part does the IT organisation play in defining and driving business strategy?	
Option	*Score*
Proactively involved in every aspect of strategic business planning	5
Proactively involved in strategic business planning in areas where IT dependency is high	4
Participates in strategic planning on a passive basis, mostly to ensure IT is kept in the loop	3
Not directly involved in strategic business planning, but has access to all of the output from it	2
Not involved in strategic planning, and simply receives instructions as a result of it	1
Question not considered relevant	0

Move responsibility for IT into the board room	
Who is considered responsible for effective delivery of value from IT?	
Option	*Score*
The main board collectively	5
The CIO sitting on the board	4
A board member to whom the CIO reports directly	3
A collective body or line of business manager to which the board has delegated responsibility	2
The IT organisation itself as a service provider, that is the board assumes no responsibility	1
Question not considered relevant	0

Develop a coherent view of the organisation that is jointly owned by the business *How comprehensive is your enterprise architecture practice?*	
Option	*Score*
Very comprehensive, both in terms of content and associated governance processes	5
Comprehensive for particularly dynamic areas of the business, but not for others	4
High-level definition only, but broadly across the business	3
High-level definition and only for selected parts of the business	2
No real definition of an enterprise architecture at this moment in time	1
Question not considered relevant	0

Develop genuine win-win partnerships with key suppliers *What is the nature of the relationship with your key suppliers?*	
Option	*Score*
Proactive win-win partnership style relationships with all of our key suppliers	5
Proactive win-win partnership style relationships with some key suppliers, but not all	4
Good working relationship with a key suppliers, but not really partnership in nature	3
Still in the process of building effective relationships with key suppliers	2
No clear definition of key suppliers at this point in time	1
Question not considered relevant	0

Institutionalise an agile alignment culture *How well are IT and business capable of remaining aligned as significant change occurs?*	
Option	*Score*
IT and business are fully aligned and both are prepared for continuous coordinated change	5
IT and business are fully aligned, and IT is prepared to follow the business swiftly as it moves	4
IT and business are mostly aligned but keeping up with business change is a challenge for IT	3
IT and business are not very well aligned, and the business is sometimes held back by IT	2
IT and business are largely misaligned, and IT is often a blocker to business change	1
Question not considered relevant	0

IT–Business alignment

Scorecard summary and planning sheet

Gain trust from the business	Current score	Target for next review
Establish a clear two-way dialogue between IT and the business		
Align expectations on the basics between IT and the business		
Achieve an acceptable level of availability and performance for all key services		
Deliver new service capability in line with promises and expectations		
Implement effective measurement and feedback mechanisms		
TOTAL		
IMPROVEMENT INITIATIVES		

Understand and reflect the business (i.e. 'tune in')	Current score	Target for next review
Establish mechanisms to coordinate goals and objectives		
Provide clear business context for significant IT-related activity		
Map the dependencies between asset, services and business value		
Balance asset and services to deliver overall business advantage		
Identify key IT suppliers		
TOTAL		
IMPROVEMENT INITIATIVES		

Engage the business	Current score	Target for next review
Make IT an integral part of the business management agenda		
Integrate IT service management into the business itself		
Implement a balanced business approach to demand management		
Embrace key IT suppliers strategically and operationally		
Institutionalise the process of sustaining alignment		
TOTAL		
IMPROVEMENT INITIATIVES		

Drive the business	Current score	Target for next review
Embrace IT as a strategic business enabler		
Move responsibility for IT into the board room		
Develop a coherent view of the organisation, jointly owned by the business		
Develop genuine win-win partnerships with key suppliers		
Institutionalise an agile alignment culture		
TOTAL		
IMPROVEMENT INITIATIVES		

OVERALL IT–BUSINESS ALIGNMENT SCORE	

Index